"Laura Petherbridge has hit a home run with *101 Tips for the Smart Stepmom*! As someone who has walked a mile in stepmom shoes, Laura accurately provides wisdom, help, and hope for any woman dating, engaged, or married to a man with kids. There's a good reason why she's called The Smart Stepmom!"

—Brenda Ockun, publisher, *StepMom Magazine*

"Across all families, a stepmom's role is among the most challenging. She is easily sabotaged, frequently confused, and often isolated. Like a warm blanket on a winter night, this book will wrap you in hope and provide practical tools for your survival toolbox. A seasoned, experienced stepmom, Laura Petherbridge is the best author and speaker I know for stepmoms; reading this book is like having her over for coffee and being mentored by her practical wisdom and insight. Buy it . . . read it . . . and share it with a friend."

—Ron L. Deal, director, FamilyLife Blended™
and bestselling author of *The Smart Stepfamily*
and *The Smart Stepdad*

"*101 Tips for the Smart Stepmom* is packed full of experiences from a stepmom who knows the excruciating pain and the exhilarating joy of embracing the role of motherhood with children she did not birth, but longs to nurture. If you have questions, the answers are here! This extraordinary resource is also excellent for Christian leaders who minister to blended families. Laura Petherbridge has written a book that every stepmom should read. Don't miss it."

—Carol Kent, speaker and author, *Unquenchable: Grow
a Wildfire Faith That Will Endure Anything* (Zondervan)

"The role of a stepmom is vital—but sometimes difficult. Laura Petherbridge offers time-tested tips and words of wisdom and encouragement to help a stepmom walk with love through the maze of blended-family living."

—Pam Farrel, coauthor of *Men Are Like Waffles, Women Are
Like Spaghetti* and author of *Becoming a Brave New Woman*

101 TIPS FOR THE SMART STEPMOM

Books by Laura Petherbridge

101 Tips for the Smart Stepmom

The Smart Stepmom
(with Ron L. Deal)

When "I Do" Becomes "I Don't"

101 TIPS FOR THE SMART STEPMOM

Expert Advice From One Stepmom to Another

LAURA PETHERBRIDGE

BETHANY HOUSE PUBLISHERS

a division of Baker Publishing Group
Minneapolis, Minnesota

Published by Bethany House Publishers
11400 Hampshire Avenue South
Bloomington, Minnesota 55438
www.bethanyhouse.com

Bethany House Publishers is a division of
Baker Publishing Group, Grand Rapids, Michigan

Printed in the United States of America

Library of Congress Cataloging-in-Publication Data
Petherbridge, Laura.
    101 tips for the smart stepmom : expert advice from one stepmom to another / Laura Petherbridge.
        pages cm
    Includes bibliographical references.
    Summary: "A parenting expert and seasoned stepmom gives practical, topically arranged advice for stepmothers"— Provided by publisher.
    ISBN 978-0-7642-1221-5 (pbk. : alk. paper)
    1. Stepmothers. 2. Parenting—Religious aspects—Christianity. 3. Remarried people—Family relationships. I. Title.
BV4529.18.P48 2014
248.8′431—dc23   2014003675

Unless otherwise indicated, Scripture quotations are from the Holy Bible, New International Reader's Version®. NIrV®. Copyright © 1995, 1996, 1998 by Biblica, Inc.™ Used by permission of Zondervan. All rights reserved worldwide. www.zondervan.com

Scripture quotations identified CEV are from the Contemporary English Version © 1991, 1992, 1995 by American Bible Society. Used by permission.

Scripture quotations identified ESV and the epigraph in chapter 3 are from The Holy Bible, English Standard Version® (ESV®), copyright © 2001 by Crossway, a publishing ministry of Good News Publishers. Used by permission. All rights reserved. ESV Text Edition: 2007

Scripture quotations identified The Message are from *The Message* by Eugene H. Peterson, copyright © 1993, 1994, 1995, 2000, 2001, 2002. Used by permission of NavPress Publishing Group. All rights reserved.

Scripture quotations identified NIV 1984 are from the HOLY BIBLE, NEW INTERNATIONAL VERSION®. Copyright © 1973, 1978, 1984 Biblica. Used by permission of Zondervan. All rights reserved.

Scripture quotations identified NLT and the epigraph in chapter 6 are from the *Holy Bible*, New Living Translation, copyright © 1996, 2004, 2007 by Tyndale House Foundation. Used by permission of Tyndale House Publishers, Inc., Carol Stream, Illinois 60188. All rights reserved.

Author is represented by Books & Such Literary Agency.

Cover design by Paul Higdon

14 15 16 17 18 19 20   7 6 5 4 3 2 1

To my mother, Roberta:

*Thank you for working so hard as a
single-parent mom to provide for Mark and me,
and for always loving and supporting me.
I love you.*

To my grandchildren, Colin and Erin:

*You are the greatest perk to being a stepmom.
I'm so grateful that God has given me the gift of—you!
Always remember, Nana loves you.*

Contents

Contents

Contents

Contents

Contents

Acknowledgments

Thank you:

Bethany House Publishers: Your compassionate heart toward stepfamilies has helped thousands become stronger. Your vision and willingness to reach out to this audience will reap vast rewards in this world and the next.

Sister stepmoms: Your willingness to share struggles, fears, hopes, wisdom, and victories makes my writing endeavors and ministry more than it could ever be without you. Personally, I am blessed more than you will ever know.

Ron Deal: Your offer to coauthor *The Smart Stepmom* opened an entire new world for me. Although in the beginning I was terrified, I am now exceedingly grateful. Thank you for seeing my potential as a stepmom mentor when I could not see it myself.

Prayer team: Your relentless, faithful, tenacious, and compassionate prayers to our heavenly Daddy undergird the strength beneath all that I do.

Precious husband, Steve: I love you for letting me use my gifts, even when it means a financial sacrifice to our family. Your support and encouragement are the reasons I am able to continue this outreach to stepfamilies. No one has ever loved me, or believed in me, like you do. I am so grateful that God sent you into my life.

Stepfamily Scott, Julie, and Colin; Todd, Jamie, and Erin: Your willingness to let me share our stepfamily journey makes it easier for me to be sincere and transparent. Even though I write the books, the expedition is a part of us all.

Glorious God: You took a suicidal, wounded, drunk, self-loathing, desperate woman and turned her into a vessel where people find help, hope, and healing. How can I ever say thank you? There are no words, so I offer you the only thing I can—my life.

Introduction

B eing a stepmom is so much more difficult than I thought it would be," stepmom Sarah shared. "I thought I was ready to take on the task of being a stepmom to my husband's three kids. But I find myself struggling with so many issues.

"Plus I feel guilty that I'm angry, sad, and frustrated all at the same time," she continued. "I snap at my husband when things aren't going well, and I feel like the wicked stepmother. What's wrong with me?"

If there is one sentence stepmoms across the globe share it's, *"Being a stepmom is so much harder than I thought it would be."* As a stepmom of more than twenty-eight years, and after many hours of life coaching, training, and helping other stepfamilies, I totally agree. There are numerous practical reasons why this is true.

During the dating process children are often more accepting of the new woman in their dad's life. She is viewed as a positive, fun friend that joins them at the zoo and trips for pizza. She brings a female touch to their dad's space and he smiles more than he did before. Life is better.

However, after a remarriage, their perspective may change, even if the child is an adult. When their dad says "I do," it's common for the kids to perceive his new partner as a threat to their relationship with him. This is when—and why—life in a stepfamily can become complicated, confusing, and chaotic.

Acknowledging and accepting what's normal is the first step toward peace and sanity. It doesn't resolve the issues, but it does neutralize the threat. Couples who pretend that stepfamily issues are the same as those in a first-time marriage are the ones in the most danger of division.

These couples often receive unwise advice from well-meaning friends, marriage experts, or church leadership. Although well-intentioned, if the mentors don't understand how second families are radically different—and extremely more complicated—than first-time families, they can throw gasoline on the fire without realizing it.

To someone with no stepfamily experience, my observations and tips may seem negative. But the woman who understands stepfamily living is nodding her head, saying, "Preach it, sister." Finding someone who can identify is a balm to her weary mind and soul. That's because stepparents—stepmoms in particular—often wear a mantle of shame when they perceive themselves as failing in their role.

When normal stepfamily bumps (okay, occasionally they are mountains) appear, thoughts of anger: "His ex-wife isn't going to dictate our house," or fear: "Will our marriage survive?" or disrespect: "My husband has no backbone when it comes to his kids," or frustration: "Is this ever going to change?" or resentment: "If that's the way it's going to be around here maybe I'll leave," can become deeply rooted.

Take heart, sweet sister stepmom, I have pondered every one of those thoughts myself. And help is on the way.

101 Tips for the Smart Stepmom provides insight to help you thrive in a stepfamily. You cannot control the other home. However, you can learn how to recognize and overcome defeating thoughts, lovingly tackle destructive cycles of unhealthy co-parenting, and address the damaging decisions made by others that threaten your home. It is possible to conquer stepfamily stress with practical tips that can "turn the *Titanic* around." Together we will build a foundation for a solid stepfamily.

Please note: Each stepmom scenario is an actual stepfamily. The names of the stepmoms and stepfamily logistics have been changed to protect their privacy and personal information.

A prayer and Bible references have been added at the end of each chapter for those who desire a deeper spiritual journey.

With a few exceptions, *101 Tips for the Smart Stepmom* avoids duplicating the issues covered in *The Smart Stepmom* coauthored with Ron Deal. Some topics, such as the ex-wife-in-law, are addressed in both books. However, the information is not the same. Although several subjects cross over into both books, if you are seeking extensive in-depth insight on a particular topic such as your own biological child, adding a new baby, discipline, or extensive co-parenting information, *The Smart Stepmom* provides specific guidance on these subjects and more.

1

Why Is It So Complicated?

Your present circumstances don't determine where you can go; they merely determine where you start.

—Nido Qubein

Now what I am commanding you today is not too difficult for you or beyond your reach.

—Moses, recorder of the
Ten Commandments

A friend and I were discussing his upcoming family vacation. He shared that his two oldest daughters were very excited, but his four-year-old would start to cry when asked if she was looking forward to flying to Michigan. Eventually, the dad asked his daughter what was wrong. She replied, "I don't know how to fly."

This is a reminder that children hear, perceive, and translate things very differently than adults.

21

The first step to obtaining a healthy stepfamily is a deeper understanding of how stepfamilies are unique and why children view them differently from their family of origin.

Tip #1 Accept That Stepfamilies Are Founded on Loss

Most couples resist hearing the root reasons why stepfamilies struggle. However, until a stepmom is willing to recognize that all stepfamilies are formed out of loss, she will continually wonder why it's an uphill battle. The refusal to accept this truth can sabotage the relationship. Once a stepmom admits that a death or divorce (or broken relationship) must have occurred for the stepfamily to form, she will begin to comprehend that stepfamilies have unique issues. Understanding this simple principle can go a long way in resolving the multifaceted matters. TV's Dr. Phil McGraw often states, "You can't change what you don't acknowledge."[1] And when it comes to stepfamilies, he couldn't be more accurate.

Tip #2 Learn Why and Where the Pain Exists

Divorce is a death—for everyone. Even if the marriage was abusive or destructive, the entire family must grieve the death of the dream, the covenant, and what "should have been." The brain of a child or teen is not yet fully developed. Therefore, they process grief differently than adults do. Author and adult child of divorce Jen Abbas explains, "At the time of our parents' divorce, we could see the physical breakup of our homes, and while we acutely felt the pain of our parents' partings, we couldn't know then how much more we would miss as we grew to understand all that home was meant to be."[2]

A smart stepmom seeks information, resources, and instruction on how the young mind works and how kids may get stuck in depression, fear, anger, and guilt. An excellent resource for adults and children is www.DC4K.org. This program provides a plethora of information as well as a support group setting for kids K–5th grade. For those in the teen years, The Landing, a program designed by Saddleback Church, is superb: www.saddlebackresources.com.

Tip #3 Embrace What's Normal

There is an erroneous expectation that when two homes merge it will immediately result in a connection between new family members. Most stepfamily experts agree that it takes approximately seven years for a stepfamily to begin to function as a bonded unit. Disappointment and feelings of failure arise when the couple presumes or demands that the children embrace new faces in the family photo.

Sometimes stepkids who do not immediately accept the new members form a connection as they get older. My brother, Mark, has two children and married a woman with two children. They had full custody of all four children ages six to eleven. They encountered numerous stressful situations in the early years of their marriage, but committed to stay the course. The kids are now in their twenties and thirties, and they sincerely view each other as siblings. The first time I heard my oldest niece, Melissa, refer to her stepbrother, Ian, as her brother, it caught me by surprise. They are living proof that with time, patience, tenacity, and wisdom some stepfamilies are able to merge into one family.

Tip #4 Recognize That Each Child Is Different

A stepmom may have one stepchild who thinks she is the greatest thing since the iPhone and another who wishes she would disappear. It's totally normal. A few determining factors can be whether they view a stepmom as a benefit or a distraction and how the child relates to the biological mother. For example, a firstborn son may feel it's his job to protect, help, and heal his mom. When a child steps into an adult role to defend or guard the mother, any kindness toward you may feel like a betrayal of her.

Age and gender are two additional factors which may cause one child to desire a relationship and the other to refrain. Teens go through seasons where they don't like any parental influence. And girls tend to perceive a stepmom as more of a threat to their relationship with their dad than boys do.

The answer is to remain available and yet guard your heart at the same time. Love the stepchild who will let you, and keep reaching out with acts of kindness toward the one who won't. It's possible that over time this child will see your good intentions.

If you are working hard to build a bridge, don't take rejection personally. When you struggle to hug the porcupine-like step-child, reread tips one through three. Then repeat these words: "It's not about me."

Tip #5 What to Do When You Feel Outside the Circle

It's not uncommon for a stepmom to feel outside the family circle. It's as if she is standing in the front yard, peering through the window, as her husband and his kids laugh and play a game together. They are the family. She is the outcast.

The husband doesn't intentionally push her outside, and he rarely perceives the setting as she does. His craving to spend time with his children and create pleasurable moments together may cause him to sacrifice or misunderstand the stepmom's feelings.

Cindi, a stepmom of four years, finally got tired of the isolation and shared with her husband, "I feel like an immature child bringing this up, but when you sit on the couch with your kids it feels as though you don't want me around. I feel like an intruder on your cozy setting. Fortunately, I've read in stepmom books that this is normal. Can we work on a few intentional ways that I could occasionally be included?"

The solution is for the couple to come up with a plan to draw the stepmom into the circle. Sometimes a secret signal between the husband and wife is necessary. This helps a husband to recognize that his wife is feeling isolated. A smart stepmom doesn't assume or blame a husband for not automatically perceiving that she is hurting. Sometimes a guy needs help connecting the dots.

Keep in mind that if the stepchildren see their dad two days per week or less, it's wise for the stepmom to remember that she sees him every day. He and his children only have a few precious hours together.

Tip #6 Encourage Your Hubby to Spend Time With His Kids

One of the biggest mistakes I made in our early stepfamily formation was not realizing how important it was for my husband to spend time alone with his sons. We immediately began doing everything together as a family. This instigated the feeling that his sons no longer had any time alone with their dad.

I experienced the same situation when I was a child. After my dad remarried a woman with two children, I rarely had any daddy-daughter time with him. Although I didn't hate my first stepmom, I did feel as if I had lost my dad to her and her children. I resented that her two sons got my father full time, and I got the crumbs.

It baffles me that I didn't consider how Steve's sons might feel when I was constantly around. This reveals how self-focused we can become and that sometimes we need others to point out the obvious.

If I had it to do over again I'd nudge my husband to spend more of his visitation time alone with his kids while I enjoyed lunch with my girlfriends.

Tip #7 Help Your Hubby Heal

How much time did your husband take to grieve the death or divorce from his first wife? Did he attend a grief or divorce recovery support group? The answers play a significant role in how ready and equipped your spouse was to enter a remarriage. It's not uncommon for a man to resist attending a support group—there are too many emotions flying around the room.

After twenty-five years in divorce recovery ministry I observed a common mistake after a divorce or death of a spouse. Most people think they are emotionally healed a lot sooner than they actually are. If an individual doesn't get the help necessary to process the various losses, it sets up the next relationship for additional problems. The unhealed person carries the decaying corpse of the last relationship into the next one. And the stench starts to resurface, infecting the new marriage.

It's never too late to get help. Resources such as DivorceCare, GriefShare, or Celebrate Recovery can provide tremendous healing.[3] It's not the wife's job to push a spouse into a recovery setting, but she can gently encourage him to recognize the underlying unresolved issues.

Tip #8 Understand That the Ex-Wife Is Here to Stay, Even if She's Gone

This crucial and potentially flammable subject is so prevalent in the life of a stepmom that I have included an entire chapter on the former spouse. However, I've added a tip here because

I want stepmoms to know I understand how often they are astonished and overwhelmed by issues from the "other home."

Accepting that there was another woman in the picture before you came along isn't enjoyable. But it is a smart stepmom's crucial step toward peace.

"Sometimes I just want to be the first," stepmom Elaine cried. "It makes me so sad that my husband has already experienced walking down the aisle, having a baby, buying a home, etc., with another woman. I know I can't change it, but it still makes me mad and frustrated."

The former spouse may have left good memories behind or a haunting exit. Either way, if the stepmom pretends the first wife didn't exist or tries to eradicate everything associated with her husband's former marriage, it's likely to create problems.

Even if the former spouse is deceased she may still have a substantial effect on the stepfamily home. And her family members are still the aunts, uncles, cousins, and grandparents to your husband's children.

Creating new "firsts" and letting go of the ones you can't reconstruct is a pivotal point.

Tip #9 Discover How to Let Go

Women typically have long memories, especially when they have been wounded. If an offense was inflicted on a stepmom by a hurting stepchild who was lashing out the only way he or she knew how, a new perspective is needed.

For the stepfamily to survive, the stepmom will need to consider these questions: *Why am I holding on to resentment and anger associated with a child's pain? If I choose to cling to this offense rather than letting it go, what will be the end result? Will holding on to this offense help or hurt my marriage? Is there a way I can protect my heart from future pain and forgive my stepchild at the same time? If my own child did something similar, would I be more willing and eager to move forward?*

I am not implying that destructive, disrespectful behavior from the kids or a spouse should be ignored. That is a different issue. I'm referring to a past offense that has been played over and over in the mind and tucked down deep for instant replay. This is an offense that is finished and needs to be forgiven.

Tip #10 Release the Guilt

My guess is that every stepmom has at least one well-meaning aunt, cousin, neighbor, co-worker, friend at church, or mother-in-law who firmly declares that a stepmom should love her husband's children exactly as she would her own. So let me lift that heavy burden of unnecessary shame off the shoulders of stepmoms everywhere. That is ridiculous.

It is very unlikely that a stepmom will have the identical connection to her husband's children as she does the baby who came out of her body, or even one she chose to adopt. When I was recording a radio show with well-respected psychologist Dr. James Dobson, he said to me, "It's unrealistic to believe you will love your husband's child exactly the same way you do your own."

When those who don't understand stepfamily living hear that statement they either scratch their heads attempting to comprehend or point a finger in judgment. However, stepmoms across the globe breathe a sigh of relief. When I get to this section of my Smart Stepmom conferences, the women in the audience often begin crying. I am vocalizing the thoughts that they are too ashamed to speak. And to make it worse, each one believes she is the only one who feels that way. To speak those thoughts out loud feels unloving, unkind, un-Jesus-like, and dare I say—wicked.

To clarify, stating that a stepmom rarely loves a stepchild the exact same way she does her own doesn't mean she is unloving.

It also doesn't give permission for her to be abusive, malicious, dismissive, negligent, or nasty.

It's highly likely that a stepmom will grow to love her stepchild. It's merely a different kind of love. A chosen love. It's a love that may take time, tears, effort, and patience to accomplish. And in many ways that makes it all the more precious.

Tip #11 Keep an Eye on Your Own Child

"My daughter came to me the other day and said that she wishes we would go back to our old house because she misses me," Carmen, a stressed stepmom, explained. "I have been spending so much time trying to make my stepkids feel at home and doing special things for them, that I didn't notice how my own child was feeling neglected."

Sometimes the complex issues surrounding the former wife, visitation schedules, and the blending of new family members can cause a stepmom to become so overwhelmed that she isn't aware of the pain her own children may be experiencing.

After the blending, it's wise to keep an eye open to changes in behavior, angry outbursts, crying, isolation, or comments about going to live with Dad. A vital step for every biological parent is to carve out ongoing one-on-one time. Validate your child's role in the family, and don't forget the hugs.

Stepmom expert Heather Hetchler shares,

> When I became a full-time stepmom, I assumed my kids were okay because they didn't say anything. However, when my oldest daughter turned eight, she said to me, "Mommy, do you love Andy and his girls more than me?" I was shocked that she would ever think such a thing. I reassured her that my remarriage did not change my love for her in any way. That conversation went a long way in helping to calm her concerns and insecurity, but if she had not spoken up I would never have known she was coping with those fears.[4]

Tip #12 Build a Bridge

Recently during a life coaching session, I encountered a stepmom who had a track record of acting negatively toward her adult stepson and his wife. They perceived her as harsh, critical, and judgmental. The stepmom admitted that her choices weren't wise. However, she proceeded to defend her actions, saying her motives were right, so she wasn't to blame. She offered an apology to the stepson, but unfortunately it was done with a prideful attitude that communicated that he and his wife needed to "get over it."

The tone in her voice revealed that she didn't grasp the gravity of her poor choices. Her decisions and pathetic apology created a gaping chasm between her husband and his son. She was more concerned about defending her position than she was building a bridge. And it was deeply affecting the marriage.

In my opinion this stepmom was clearly wrong. And I told her so. She assumed I would wave a stepmom banner and say her husband should defend his wife's position. But her arrogance and adamant refusal to admit she was wrong, take ownership for the pain she had caused, and do what was necessary to restore the relationship made that impossible.

Marriage only works when each spouse is willing to acknowledge a mistake, attempt to rectify the offense, and then do what is necessary to restore trust.

Tip #13 Avoid the "D" Word

"I used to make comments such as, 'You are lucky I'm still here' and 'Most women in my position might be gone by now' in the midst of a fight," stepmom Holly explained. "My husband finally said, 'Don't ever say something like that again unless you are prepared to leave. I can't take the what ifs.' At that moment God convicted me and revealed that I was wanting the pain to end, not my marriage. I then understood that I was doing serious damage to my husband and my marriage by making empty threats."

When a marriage is constantly threatened by divorce, the trust and the bond between husband and wife breaks down. I advise couples to make a vow together that the word *divorce* is forbidden. If your spouse refuses to make this commitment, be the first to set the example. The only tongue you can control is your own.

Tip #14 Create a Spa for the Soul

It's wise to remember that a stepfamily has seasons of growth, joy, struggles, and excitement just like any other family. The next time a challenge arises, try what I call a Spa for the Soul. One or more of the following steps can help to ease the stress: take a deep whiff of your favorite scent, go for a walk, make an "I'm thankful for" list, read a Bible verse, or pray for someone else who is hurting. This may minimize the immediate stress of the situation.

Ask yourself: "When I look back one week, one month, one year from now, will I consider this issue/battle worth my time, stress, gray hair, and wrinkles? Will I wonder why I viewed it as such a stressful or fearful thing? Will I wish I had let it go, or will I be proud of the way I tackled the problem?"

If you desire to attend a stepmom retreat, I host several each year along with a team of stepmoms. For more information, visit www.SisterhoodofStepmoms.com.

‿○‿

Lord, I need your help. I thank you that you are always available to me. You know my needs before I even speak them. I never have to worry if you lack the interest or if you are too busy to hear my requests. You are for me— not against me. When stepfamily complexities attempt to overwhelm my thoughts, my emotions, and my world, teach me how to trust you. Help me to remember that there is no situation that is so intense that your peace cannot penetrate. And I humbly ask for your transforming love, grace, and mercy to permeate my home. Thank you for your faithfulness in each and every circumstance.

Suggested Bible verses:
Psalm 42:5; Philippians 4:13; Hebrews 13:6; 1 John 5:14–15

2

When Your Hubby Is Stuck: Stepmom Frustration

Your spouse is not your enemy.

—Dennis Rainey

Where you go I will go, and where you stay I will stay.
Your people will be my people and your God my God.

—Ruth, an ancestor
to Jesus Christ

My husband lets his kids walk all over him. It's nauseating," stepmom Sheila declared. "If I say anything about it, he snaps at me like I'm the one doing something wrong. I'd like his kids to be respectful. Is that so wrong? I don't understand why I'm the bad guy when all I'm trying to do is help him raise decent kids."

And stepmoms across the world reply, "Amen, sister."

I was raised in a very strict single-parent home. My idea of how children should speak, behave, and respond to a parent was formed by my mom's example of child rearing. I'm not saying all of what I observed and experienced was healthy or wise. However, my brother and I were very good kids who got into little trouble. Disrespect or disobedience toward my mom or any other adult was met with severe consequences.

When I naïvely strolled into a stepfamily, I brought with me all my preconceived parenting thoughts. And here's the rub: They aren't my kids. If I wanted to raise my own children in the same manner and with the same standards, that would be my prerogative. But my husband's kids aren't my kids.

What's a stepmom to do? Here are a few tips. If you need more, *The Smart Stepmom* has two full chapters on parenting written for the couple to read together. Advice from someone outside of the marriage can help to break the ice when the issues become tense.

Tip #15 Look at His Single-Parenting Days

While you were dating your husband, did you notice that he was a pushover when it came to his kids? Was there a little red flag that you chose to ignore boldly waving over that scenario, proclaiming, "Watch and observe closely"? If you are like most stepmoms, the answer is a resounding—Yes!!

And yet when we women marry this pushover dad, we are shocked, frustrated, and angry that he has a hard time saying no to his kids. Why did we think a wedding ring would change his parenting style?

A significant step to unraveling this issue is for a stepmom to take a deep look into why she ignored the red flag. Why would a woman believe that remarriage would instantly cure her husband of enabling and transform him into a better or more disciplined dad?

Before blaming her husband, a stepmom needs to unearth her unrealistic response to a major issue that was clearly present when she stepped into her husband's life. When we ignore issues that are obvious, it's necessary to discover why. Resources such as *Changes That Heal* by Cloud and Townsend can help tremendously and may serve as a springboard to address the root reasons for the denial.

Tip #16 Is Your Husband Parenting out of Fear or Guilt?

After more than twenty-five years of working with single parents and stepfamilies, one of the biggest and most common mistakes I've observed is parenting out of guilt or fear rather than from a stable foundation. Fathers in particular feel a tremendous burden to automatically have the knowledge, ability, and financial resources to solve every problem.

When a dad observes how divorce has affected his children, he often feels helpless. And if he was the one who initiated the marital breakup, his response may intensify.

A stepmom cannot change the way her husband parents. But she can help him to discover the reasons he is lenient and attempting to appease every whim. Abigail Van Buren (Dear Abby) says it this way: "If you want children to keep their feet on the ground, put some responsibility on their shoulders."

Presenting teachable options before him and then stepping away without nagging or pushing is the best move. A few suggestions include a local parenting class and resources such as *Boundaries with Kids* by Cloud and Townsend or *Have a New Kid by Friday* by Dr. Kevin Leman. Seeking professional counseling from a therapist who specializes in kids can also help.

Tip #17 "What If It Were MY Child?"

I remember the first time I asked myself one of a stepmom's hardest questions.

My husband, Steve, was very hurt over something his son did. It was an act of negligence that cut deeply. However, as soon as he spoke with his son on the phone, his anger dissipated. In an instant all was forgiven. He didn't even mention the issue to him.

I was angry and wanted to tell my stepson how he had hurt his father. That's when a little voice in my head probed, "Remember a few months ago when your loved one hurt you so badly? You cried for days, Laura. But then you quickly forgave her insensitivity. Why do you think it's wrong for Steve to do the same thing?"

Yikes! I realized that the next time I felt my husband should be harsher with his kids, a good litmus test would be to ask myself the question, "What if it were *my* child?"

Suddenly I saw it through a different lens.

Tip #18 Explore How Your Hubby Was Parented

How does a person learn to parent? Unless they attend classes or see a therapist, they tend to follow the pattern set by their parents. This was either a good role model or a bad one.

"My father-in-law is a very cruel and harsh man," stepmom Danelle explained. "My husband doesn't talk about his childhood much, but on occasion he explains the beatings he got as a kid. He says his father did it to toughen him up and make him a man," she continued.

"I have kids from my first marriage. My husband sets a very high standard of how they should behave. It's unrealistic. However, when parenting his own kids he is the opposite. He lets them do whatever they want. It's as if he is afraid to say no to them."

Danelle's husband is a classic example of a father who didn't have a good parenting example. His emotions dictate the standard. The short fuse he exhibits towards his stepkids is patterned after how he was parented. He blows up at them. But with his own children, he has no idea how to set healthy boundaries and consequences.

This is a dad who desperately needs to obtain information on what constructive, encouraging, fruitful parenting looks like.

A wife cannot force her husband to dig up past pain. But if he chooses, he can find help from the resources previously mentioned.

Tip #19 Research How Children Cope With Loss

It's very hard to admit that our children have been wounded by divorce or death. We passionately long to believe that they will get over the issue quickly and that the impact on them will be minimal. However, studies such as the *New York Times* bestseller *The Unexpected Legacy of Divorce: The 25 Year Landmark Study* by Wallerstein, Lewis, and Blakeslee and *Between Two Worlds: The Inner Lives of Children of Divorce* by Elizabeth Marquardt clearly reveal the opposite. Wallerstein explains,

> When I began studying the effects of divorce on children and parents in the early 1970s, I, like everyone else, expected them to rally. But as time progressed, I grew increasingly worried that divorce is a long-term crisis that was affecting the psychological profile of an entire generation. I caught glimpses of this long-term effect in my research that followed the children into late adolescence and early adulthood, but it's not until now—when the children are fully grown—that I can finally see the whole picture. Divorce is a life-transforming experience. After divorce, childhood is different. Adolescence is different. Adulthood—with the decision to marry or not and have children or not—is different. Whether the final outcome is good

or bad, the whole trajectory of an individual's life is profoundly altered by the divorce experience.[1]

Even though it's hard to hear what kids of divorce or loss are experiencing, parents and stepparents will be much better equipped to help them if they learn why the children are hurting, how long they need to grieve, productive action steps to help them process the loss, and management skills.

Merely taking the steps to learn reveals to the husband, the children, and other family members that the stepmom desires to understand and have compassion for her stepkids.

Tip #20 Encourage; Don't Emasculate

Confession is good for the soul—so here goes.

Sometimes I have a sharp, condescending tongue. And I hate it. There are times when the words I spew out belittle, disrespect, and emasculate my husband. I view it as my greatest shame and flaw. I have begged God to heal me, and with his massive wisdom, generosity, and patience I've made progress.

Several years ago God revealed to me how my words were affecting my sweet husband. One time I observed Steve's face as what I said reduced him to rubble. His anguished expression pierced my own heart. I realized that my sinful momentary pleasure of words said in haste had deeply hurt him. My words were creating walls of pain and shame in our marriage.

My tongue seemed to be out of control, with a life and mind of its own. With God's help I learned how to think before I spoke and express my anger or frustration in a way that was beneficial to our relationship. I learned how to communicate through a different method, tone, and attitude.

On occasion, when I'm in a bad mood, hungry, or frustrated, I still slip and wicked words fly. But I'm much better at encouraging my husband and not emasculating him than I used to be.

The next time you decide to speak in anger, check your hubby's face. Is that tongue lashing, which feels so good in the moment, producing the results you desire? If not, know that God is more than willing to help you learn how to tame your tongue. Reading the Bible verses in James chapter three can provide strength.

Tip #21 Set Healthy Boundaries

"My stepdaughter, Kayla, needs to take medication in the morning," explained Brianna. "Since her dad leaves for work shortly before she gets up for school, it became my job to make certain she takes it. Every morning turned into a nightmare as I tried begging, pleading, bribing, and sometimes threatening her in order to get the medicine down.

"Finally, I stepped back," she continued. "I calmly and gently spoke to my husband and said, 'This isn't working. Kayla refuses to take the medicine for me and I won't fight with her anymore. She will need to get up a few minutes early so that you are the one helping her take her medication. It's not that I don't care, and I'm not being miserable about it, I just can't do it anymore.'"

The next day Brianna's husband got his daughter up and told her to take the pill. She started to balk and her dad responded, "Kayla, I have to leave for work, and you have to take this medicine. Now swallow it." And she did.

Part of becoming a smart stepmom is learning when it's necessary to set healthy, loving boundaries. Saying no isn't about being abrasive, nasty, condescending, or cruel. It's simply allowing the person who should be taking responsibility to do so.

Perhaps in your stepfamily it's your husband who needs to learn how to say no. When a father enters a remarriage there is one rule that should be implemented and never changed. He needs to set this boundary with his children: "You do not have to like your stepmom, you do not have to love your stepmom, but you do have to treat your stepmom with dignity and respect. This is my bride. I stood before God and made a vow to love, honor, cherish, and respect her as long as I live. That includes not allowing you to treat her with disrespect. You are my child and I love you with all of my heart. I will never leave you. But I will not allow you to speak disrespectfully to my wife. If you do, _____ will be the consequence."

The consequence may vary depending on the age and the relationship with the child. Understand it's likely that children—even adult children—will test their dad to determine if he is serious. When a husband allows anyone—including his children—to treat his wife in a disrespectful manner, it erodes the marital foundation and instills a lack of trust. This robs the intimacy, love, compassion, and mutual accountability that is mandatory for a marriage to survive and thrive.

Tip #22 Learn What Hill to Die On

"My husband and I are healthy eaters, and I'm a vegetarian," stepmom Brenda declared. "I think it's horrible that his kids eat fast food and drink gallons of soda. So when they visit us I insist that we have organic, healthy food.

"Recently his kids have threatened to stop visiting us if they can't have the food they like, and my husband is thinking about backing down on this issue. If he gives in to them, I'm going to stop cooking altogether and he will be sleeping on the couch."

Although this stepmom's motives are right, her methods might be wrong.

In stepfamilies, it's important to determine what "hill to die on." Another way of saying it: Choose your battles wisely. Things such as disrespect, swearing, violence, stealing, disregard for another's feelings or space, damaging your home, and under-age drinking are examples of things that should be on that hill. These are crucial issues.

If this stepmom makes food her crusade, is she winning the battle but losing the war? If the kids refuse to visit because she won't allow them to have hot dogs and Pepsi, and that causes a division between her husband and his kids—is it worth it? Or would allowing a bag of Doritos be a better option?

And more important, will her husband resent her in the long run? Will he blame her for the compound fracture in the relationship with his children?

There might be a way to compromise. She could buy healthier chips and treats that might not be her first choice, but it would show she cares. Her husband could take the kids out for burgers and have one-on-one time with them, and she can enjoy a salad with her girlfriends.

If she doesn't make this a hill to die on, but rather gently nudges them toward trying delicious oven-baked sweet potato fries rather than deep fried, it could eventually bring peace and healthy eating for everyone. That way the kids won't feel that she is dictating every meal, and their dad's every move.

If this stepmom refuses to accept that these are not her children, they have a mother who is in charge of their eating habits, and they live in another home that has different guidelines, she will have tofu in the refrigerator but will likely have lost everything else.

The food battle may be won, but the war for the relationship with her stepkids, peace in the home, and a healthy marriage may be lost.

Emotions may take over, and sometimes it is difficult to determine what "hill to die on." A wise third party can help to provide an unbiased, beneficial perspective.

Tip #23 Communicate Productively

When I was twelve my best friend and I were attempting to maneuver my bike down a flight of stairs. I kept aggressively telling her the right way to do it, and she was frustrated. Finally, she tired of my demeaning orders and dropped the bike, saying, "Forget it." Then she went home. That was the day I realized I'm too bossy. And that people don't respond well to bullying.

During my training to become a life coach, I was taught how to help a person discover for themselves the answers they are seeking. One of the best ways to communicate effectively is to ask questions. Jesus did it all the time. "What do you want me to do for you?" (Matthew 20:32), "Why do you call me, 'Lord, Lord,' and still don't do what I say?" (Luke 6:46), "Who do you say I am?" (Matthew 16:15). Now instead of telling Steve what he should do (of course, I'm right about everything), I ask him questions that prompt his mind to consider different options.

When your husband feels discouraged about a disconnection with his child, instead of saying, "I think you should _____," try asking questions.

"What do you think communicates love to your son? What makes him smile?" or "Do you think Joshua would like it if just the two of you went to the ball game together?" or "Did you hear Joshua mention the car show in town next week? A love of cars seems to be something the two of you have in common. Do you think he might like to go?"

Pray for ways to ask strategic questions. You will be amazed at how creative thinking in this manner brings about results.

Tip #24 Help Your Hubby Articulate

Some stepmoms are the communication vehicle between the ex-wife-in-law and their husband. If the stepmom is able to keep peace between the two homes without becoming caught in the tug-of-war, this can be a good solution. On the other end of the spectrum is the ex-spouse who refuses to even acknowledge that her children have a stepmom. Either situation pushed to an extreme can place tremendous pressure and angst on a stepmom.

There is no cookie-cutter answer to stepfamily communication complexities. To keep tempers from flaring, it's sometimes a good idea to limit the communication to factual and data-based email. Just remember that anything in writing (email, text, letters, etc.) can be used in court. Avoid using Facebook, Twitter, or any other social media to communicate with a former spouse. It is too easy for private information to be viewed by others.

Whenever possible the stepmom's goal should be to help her husband communicate with the kids and former spouse, rather than exacerbating the situation. If a stepmom is furious about a problem, badgering her husband to stand up to his ex usually fails to accomplish the desired outcome.

I am not implying that a stepmom should roll over and play dead. I am saying that offering suggestions on how he can communicate more effectively with his ex will go much further, and keep everyone's blood pressure down!

Tip #25 Stop Stepping Into Your Husband's Role— Even if He Won't Step Up

"My husband constantly tells me that I am better at parenting his kids than he is," stepmom Marcy verbalized. "Although I'm grateful that he sees me as a good mother to his children, and I don't mind helping him, I feel like he dumps the responsibility on me."

Many women naturally fall into the role of mother. And it's not uncommon for a husband to step away from his parenting job and abdicate the responsibility to his wife—if she lets him.

This is a situation where the stepmom needs to calmly explain to her husband that she is eager to help him co-parent, but she is not willing to take on the entire responsibility.

During this discussion she needs to clearly present the specific ways she feels "dumped on." This should be done with kindness not accusation, with very specific guidelines and examples. Most men are willing to learn how to become a better father; they just need help.

For the husband who refuses to hear his wife's concerns, a stronger approach will be necessary. She may need to take several steps back and allow the parenting duties to fall into his lap naturally. When he realizes that his wife is standing firm on this issue, it may turn into an argument. When setting a healthy boundary it often gets worse for a short season of time before it gets better. This is normal. Chapter 10 provides additional insight into how to set healthy boundaries.

Tip #26 Decide Whether You Want to Be Right— Or Married

Did you ever notice that it's all right for you to say something negative about a family member, but if someone else makes the same comment the claws come out? This anomaly also applies to your husband and his kids.

Early in our marriage when my husband would say something objective or mention a flaw in one of his sons, I assumed that gave me permission to say something similar.

I was wrong. Even if I made the exact same comment about his children, he didn't like it. It has been extremely difficult, and I learned the hard way, but when it comes to negative statements about his kids I need to zip my lip.

That doesn't mean I don't make suggestions or bring up a subject that may be difficult or uncomfortable. But whenever

I'm tempted to say something that might come across as critical or unfavorable, I take a step back and rethink my thoughts. I've learned to ponder these three questions before opening my mouth: "Is it true? Is it kind? Is it necessary?" I normally can get past the first two, but the third one usually shuts me up fairly quickly.

Sometimes marriage requires that we choose peace (not enabling or people pleasing, that's a perversion of peace) over being right. It is very possible that a stepmom has the correct viewpoint and perspective about a certain situation. However, in order to keep the marriage strong she may need to let go of the desire to prove her point.

Tip #27 Accept That the Church Might Not Be Equipped

If you turn to your church for advice, the classes they provide are normally geared for first-time families. This may add to stepfamily frustration because parenting and co-parenting between two homes is radically different than in first-time families. As I was writing this chapter I received an email from a compassionate woman who sought help from church leadership. She was devastated by their response. Instead of helping her to navigate the complex waters of stepfamily living, they chastised her for not being a more loving stepmom.

It is possible that this church is merely uninformed and oblivious to the differences between first-time marriages and stepfamilies. Feel free to share the following tips with your church about why the typical parenting guidelines don't work in a stepfamily.

- In a stepfamily the biological parent should be the key disciplinarian. It normally takes several years for the trust and bond between the child and stepparent to form. Any attempt by the biological parent or stepparent to rush the bond usually backfires. This is why it is unwise for the stepparent (including a stepdad) to immediately assume an authoritarian role over a stepchild.

- The child is often in each home 50 percent of the time or less, making it more difficult to implement boundaries.
- The rules between the two homes are normally different. This causes confusion for the child when something is permissible in one home, but not the other.
- The child has two parents and may also have two stepparents, plus a plethora of extended family giving the child instructions. All of these adults likely view their parenting style as the right one.
- When a parent remarries someone who has children it typically changes the child's birth order. This is partly why many children struggle in this new setting. Therefore, parenting takes on a different dynamic as the child adjusts to an unfamiliar role in the family.
- Parenting children who are grieving is radically different from parenting those who have not experienced trauma.

∽o∾

Lord, I long to be a support system for my husband. Help me to learn what to do with my frustrations and anger when he is not following through as I believe he should be. Teach me how to see him through your eyes.

Give me wisdom to discern when I should open my mouth and when to keep silent. I know that I am accountable to you for every thought that I think and the words that I speak. Holy Spirit, guide me on how to relate to my spouse, my children, my stepchildren, extended family members, and others. Grant me patience when I'm at my wits' end. Show me the difference between speaking the truth in love and ranting because I need to get things off my chest. I am not called to be a doormat or to ignore toxic situations in my home. Therefore, I need your help to discover the difference between wisely stepping away from the chaos and being a people pleaser.

I love my husband. I don't want to lose respect for him. Today I commit a new dedication to my spouse, my vows, and the role I play in helping this stepfamily survive and thrive.

Suggested Bible verses:
Ecclesiastes 4:9–10; Proverbs 27:17; Ephesians 4:31–32; Luke 21:15

3

Will We Ever Get Along?— The Ex-Wife-in-Law

Self-pity is a slimy, bottomless pit. Once you fall in, you tend to go deeper and deeper into the mire. As you slide down those slippery walls, you are well on your way to depression, and the darkness is profound.

—Sarah Young

Let every person be quick to hear, slow to speak, slow to anger.

—The apostle James, half-brother to Jesus Christ

M om says I shouldn't love you as much as I love her," the stepdaughter whispered to her stepmom.

"You are the luckiest girl in the whole world," the stepmom responded. "You have a mom who loves you so much and would do anything for you. And you have me, who loves you to the moon and back again and the stars and back again. The best

49

part about that is, you can love your mom with all your heart, and I will love you for the rest of your life."

"I love you to the moon and stars and back too," the child replied.[1]

Now that's one smart stepmom! She did what was best for the child rather than react out of frustration and annoyance toward the biological mom—not an easy task. Hands down, the most common frustration for most stepmoms is when, where, and how to work alongside the former spouse, a.k.a. ex-wife-in-law. Numerous factors come into play when making decisions regarding this relationship.

For the sake of the children, some moms are willing to work together in harmony with a stepmom. Other moms are too angry, selfish, hurt, or unstable to take the steps necessary to walk toward peace.

The Smart Stepmom explores the various types of biological moms. As you might imagine, it covers a lot of territory and can provide a more in-depth understanding of each mother.

Tip #28 Reverse the Roles

Ask your husband how he feels when his kids are introduced to the biological mom's new boyfriend. Look deep into his eyes as he describes the raw pain of watching another man play a father role in his kids' lives. Observe your husband as he reveals his fears regarding this man and whether he will be good to his kids or harm them. Watch his fury when another man gets to take his son to football or drive his daughter to the prom. And recognize the rage when his son or daughter calls this new man Daddy.

How does that feel? Most stepmoms experience tremendous sorrow as they watch their sweet spouse struggle, grieve, and weep over the loss of control and the new unwanted parental influence that divorce and remarriage naturally bring.

In order to be a smart stepmom, it helps to remember that everything I just described about your husband's experience is exactly how his ex-wife feels when she thinks of you. Nelson Mandela offers excellent advice that applies to communicating with the former spouse: "If you talk to a man in a language he understands, that goes to his head. If you talk to him in his language, that goes to his heart."

Even if she is an unstable mother or the one who chose to end the former marriage, it hurts or causes fear when she thinks of another woman stepping into the lives of her children.

Tip #29 Repeat After Me: "You Can't Control Her"

"I have two young stepsons," Lucinda shared. "When they arrive at our home, it's obvious they haven't had a bath in days. Their clothes and hair are filthy and their nails haven't been cleaned or clipped. They tell us that they eat fast food all the time and rarely have a home-cooked meal. I can't stand what a horrible mother she is to them."

It's hard on a stepmom when she feels the kids are not receiving the parental care they deserve. It usually leads to thinking they would be better off in her home, and that might be true. But it's not reality. And it merely leads to frustration and anger toward the mom over issues that likely aren't going to change.

Accepting that you cannot control what goes on in the other home is a crucial part of obtaining stepfamily peace. Obviously, abuse or severe neglect must be addressed immediately. But the normal stuff that the mom either neglects to do or does differently than the dad or stepmom would do must be released. Now would be a good time for a reminder of the serenity prayer.

The Serenity Prayer by Reinhold Niebuhr
God, give us grace to accept with serenity the things that cannot be changed, courage to change the things that should be changed, and the wisdom to distinguish the one from the other.[2]

Tip #30 Acknowledge That She Is the Mom

Because being a stepmom often includes all the duties of a biological mom, such as dishes, laundry, homework assistance, cooking, hugs, tears, and Band-Aids to wounded knees, it's easy to fall into the trap of assuming you have all the parental rights over the child.

"My ex-husband's new wife shows up at every school function and parent teacher conference," a mom proclaimed. "She even asked the teacher to add her name as one of the parental helpers in my daughter's classroom. I understand she is married to my ex-husband, and she plays a significant role in the life of my children. What I don't understand is why she feels this gives her permission to step in and parent my child."

This is a double-edged sword. On the one hand, a stepmom has all the tasks of being a mom, but in reality she doesn't have the rights of being a mom. Do you doubt me? Ask yourself this question: "If my husband died, do I have any visitation or legal rights to his children?" Unless you are a full-time stepmom who has legally adopted his children, the answer is no.

I think stepmoms could benefit from asking themselves, "Who is this child's mother?" I totally understand how difficult it is when you give your heart, soul, and time to a child who isn't your own. But often it's necessary for a stepmom to take a step back and reflect, "Even though I have grown to love this child, he or she isn't my child but my husband and his former wife's child. This child already has a mother. And it is not me!"

Tip #31 Clarify Your Intentions

"I was sensing that my husband's ex-wife was worried that I was trying to push her away as the mother," stepmom Samantha shared. "So I decided to speak with her. She reluctantly joined me for coffee. I explained that in no way was I trying to replace her. I shared that I respect her role as the mother, I am their dad's wife, and my goal is to help the children adjust to stepfamily life as much as possible.

"I explained that she has great kids that any mom would be very proud to have, and if there is anything I can do to help them I'm willing to try," she continued. "She seemed genuinely surprised and taken aback. I think she thought I was going to cause a fight and stir up trouble. But I have no desire to get into drama if it can be avoided."

This stepmom gets it. She noticed that the mom was uncomfortable with her role in the lives of her kids, and she took action to diffuse the bomb before it exploded. She revealed good intentions and explained that she isn't a threat. This stepmom has no desire to usurp the mother's role, or be a mommy to kids who already have one. In addition, she praised the mom for having good children and offered to help.

Obviously, if the mother is unwilling to communicate with the stepmom, a face-to-face meeting isn't possible. In that case, it's best to put those things in a short, simple note. But remember, anything in an email, text, or written format can be used in a court of law. So patiently review what you write. In addition, your husband should be fully aware of the communication, and it's a good idea to have a friend, fellow stepmom, or divorce recovery leader take a peek at the note before you send it.

Tip #32 Communicate Clearly With Your Husband

"It feels like my husband's ex-wife runs our home," stepmom Holly lamented. "She dictates so much of our schedule, and my husband doesn't want to rock the boat so he goes along with her. My opinion is ignored and I get so frustrated."

One of the difficult issues of being a stepmom is learning how to recognize and accept what is normal stepfamily stuff that can't be changed and when to put your foot down. There is no easy cookie-cutter answer or formula for this complexity. Each situation is unique. The problem comes when a stepmom refuses to accept that there are going to be some situations she (and her husband) cannot control.

What she can control is the communication with her sweet hubby. Telling him that she needs to be heard and exactly how he can show that he's listening to her is key.

A man can't read a woman's mind. Most husbands tell me they would prefer that their wives clearly spell out what they are thinking rather than drop hints. Discussing solutions together helps the stepmom know that her husband cares. In Holly's situation, it would be beneficial for her to explain to her husband the need for him to communicate with her before he agrees to let his former spouse change the schedule. It will go a long way in their marriage if he calls, saying, "Hi, Sweetheart. Susan's boss has asked her to work late, and I know we normally wouldn't get the kids tonight, and it changes our plans, but I'd really like to do that. I promise just the two of us will do something after they leave. Would that be okay with you?"

This will open the door of conversation. Often the stepmom will need to say yes and change her plans to accommodate his kids. This is part of stepfamily living, especially if the kids are young. But sometimes a dad will need to tell his ex-wife no. This is where things get tense and even ugly. Each circumstance should be evaluated and discussed so that neither spouse feels that they are the only one making a compromise.

Tip #33 Prepare for Difficult Situations or Lies

"My mom said if my dad would pay his child support instead of taking care of you and your kids we could go on a vacation," ten-year-old Kourtney stated to her stepmom.

"Grrrrr," the stepmom roared.

After a remarriage it is important to learn how to respond when the kids believe or hear something that isn't true. That issue typically surrounds money and/or child support.

First, I need to stress that the steps to resolution should be taken by the dad, *not* the stepmom. If the stepmom is present during the discussion, she should let her husband do all the talking. The child needs to know this information is coming from the biological parent—the one they are bonded to and trust—not from the stepmom. The child often views the stepmom as the reason why the money isn't coming in and believes that she is preventing their father from paying.

Hear this clearly: If the stepmom does the talking, it will solidify the child's and former spouse's conviction that the dad is a puppet on a string dancing to whatever tune his wife desires. It paints the stepmom as the villain.

If the child asks the stepmom questions directly, the response should be something such as "Kourtney, I'm sorry your parents' divorce has caused you to think about adult issues, because kids should be kids. When your father comes home we can all talk about it together. You must be hungry after a long day at school. Would you like a snack?" This reveals that you have addressed the issue, but that the conversation is over until Dad comes home.

When attempting to replace a lie with the truth, there are a few guidelines. In an age-appropriate manner, with compassion and patience, and without anger, your husband should:

- Explain that this is an adult issue: "Kourtney, I'm sorry that you have been drawn into the discussion about money between your mom and me. This is an adult issue, not something a ten-year-old should worry about."
- Identify with the pain: "I know these issues are confusing for you. It must be hard to know which parent is telling the truth when we say conflicting things. You didn't ask to be from a divorced home, and I'm so sorry."

- Speak truth: "Kourtney, I want you to know that as your dad I love you. I want to tell you the truth. I know your mom says that I don't pay the child support, but that isn't true. I'm not saying your mom is a bad person. I know she loves you. I don't know why she is saying this, but as your dad I must tell you the truth."

- Offer proof: "If you would like to look at my bank statements, which show how much I'm paying your mom, I am willing to show them to you. If that makes you uncomfortable, you don't need to look at them. But I'm offering a way to show you that I'm telling the truth."

- Move on: "Kourtney, I want what is best for you. As your dad I am paying my child support, but even more important, I want you to know how deeply I love you. Try not to worry yourself over adult issues. If your mom brings them up, it's okay to tell her you don't want to talk about it."

- Provide affirmation and security: "Honey, even though I'm remarried, I'm always here if you want to talk about anything. You don't need to be afraid to ask me."

This should help the child relax and know the documents are available if she wants to see them. Some children will want the proof; others will not. Your husband's offer may be enough to quell the turmoil.

If a father refuses to have a talk like this with his child, that doesn't mean the stepmom should step into his role. This is between parent and child. And he must suffer the long-term consequences if he is unwilling to face this issue.

Tip #34 Pay What Was Promised

Here is a part many stepmoms don't want to hear, but if sanity, integrity, and virtue are to be found it's necessary. When your husband decided to get remarried, that didn't eliminate his responsibility to provide emotionally, financially, physically, and spiritually for the children from his first family. The alimony and child support from his divorce agreement are still due, whether you agree with it or not.

That doesn't mean he is supposed to be a bank and give in to his child's every manipulative whim. It doesn't mean he should jump every time his ex-wife wants something. Please don't hear what I'm *not* saying. He needs to be committed and pay what he is legally required to contribute. If his job has changed and the income is less, that is a different story. Legal counsel will be necessary to change the divorce agreement.

Numerous stepmoms believe that when a dad gets remarried and takes on a second family, his first set of children should have compassion and understanding about the financial strain of two homes. This is incorrect. He brought those children into the world, and he is still fully responsible to provide for them. In addition, he signed a legal divorce agreement making a vow that he would deliver. It is his duty and obligation. He gave his word.

My husband is an extremely honest and truthful man. He always paid his child support and all the doctor, dentist, etc., bills early. (He was a banker for twenty-five years, which should explain why.) And we still had financial battles with his former spouse. It's just one of the unfortunate consequences of divorce.

Tip #35 Don't Throw Gasoline on the Fire

One woman shared, "I am engaged to a man who is not yet divorced. He is constantly going to court over legal issues. I want to be supportive, and he wants me by his side so that his ex-wife will know he has moved on."

Unless the goal is to antagonize an already volatile situation, I would highly recommend that a fiancée or a stepmom avoid the courtroom, as her presence will only make the situation worse. Lara R. Badain, Esq., explains it this way:

> If you want to save yourself unnecessary legal headaches, excessive attorney fees and a long drawn-out process, don't rub your ex-wife's nose in your new relationship. The litigation process is stressful enough. Why make it more so? While this may seem obvious, you'd be surprised at how many fathers show up to court appearances with their new girlfriends in tow.[3]

A stepmom needs to avoid things that exacerbate the problem. Sometimes we want our presence known, or there is a desire for the former spouse to see us with "our man." But that usually backfires. The less we intentionally aggravate the mother of his children the better it will be for everyone.

Tip #36 Overcome Evil With Good

Have you ever considered doing something nice for your stepchild's mother? My mom always says, "You draw more bees with honey than you do with vinegar." The Bible says it this way: "Don't pay back evil with evil. Don't pay back unkind words with unkind words. Instead, pay them back with kind words. That's what you have been chosen to do. You can receive a blessing by doing it" (1 Peter 3:9). Did you notice the end result of choosing not to insult another person? God says when we refrain from inflicting an insult we reap a blessing upon ourselves. Maybe you've never thought about that before.

What if a stepmom took the first step to do something on Mother's Day or the biological mom's birthday that communicates "Let's work on this together"? It takes a mature person to take the first step toward mending a fractured communication. I'm not implying that you become trusted friends or go to the spa together. But what if the stepmom was the first one to lay down her sword? Perhaps a note stating:

> *Dear _____ ,*
>
> *I know in the past we haven't always seen eye to eye, but I desire to work together to make things easier for the children.* (Note to stepmom: Do not use the phrase "our children," as this is often inflammatory.) *Couldn't we start over? I am willing to do my part to ease the tension between us. Life is too short to spend it fighting all the time.*
>
> *Please accept this small gift as my way of saying I'm sorry for the times I didn't take the time to look at the situation from your point of view. I know you love your kids and that you are a good mom. Can't we come to a compromise for their sake?*
>
> *Sincerely,*

She may refuse. She may laugh in your face. She may make fun of you on Facebook. But guess what? You will be the one who can lay her head on the pillow at night and know you did your part to attempt peace with the mother of your stepkids. And your husband will see the emotional risk you took for his kids. She may reject your offer, but I assure you it will speak volumes of love to your husband and his children.

Tip #37 You Can't Fix Crazy

"I feel so sorry for my stepkids," stepmom Julie shared. "Their mom is really irrational and peculiar. They never know what is coming next. One minute she is supermom, baking cupcakes and helping with homework; the next she is screaming and throwing a tantrum because they left a dirty dish in the living room.

"She is the same way with my husband," she continued. "He calls one day and she is thrilled to let him take the kids an extra day, and goes on and on about what a great dad he is. A week later she won't let him see them at all and tells the kids, and anyone else who will listen, that he is a deadbeat dad. We never know what to expect."

It's possible this ex-wife has a mental issue or at the very least an erratic emotional state. Unless your husband feels his children are in physical or emotional danger, there isn't much you can do to fix the situation. Creating stability in your home reveals to the stepchildren that it is possible to have a home free of chaos and eccentric behavior. Respond to their comments with compassion: "Joshua, I'm sorry your mom's mood swings hurt and confuse you. I don't think she means to make it difficult for you. Always know your dad and I want you to be safe and secure, and we are here for you. If you are scared or sad you can always call us." If the child is old enough, and they know that the mom takes medication, it might be wise to add, "It's possible your mom forgot to take her medicine and that's why she is acting that way." This will help to explain that it's not the child's fault.

Tip #38 Learn That Hurt People, Hurt People

I was once an extremely wounded woman. I didn't even realize how those injuries to my soul affected my relationships. On the outside everything looked fine. I appeared confident, happy, and productive. But on the inside I was filled with self-loathing, fear, and shame. And that cycle of destruction took its toll. It led me to drink heavily in an effort to numb the pain, and it produced hurtful words and actions toward others in an attempt to protect my maimed heart from further attacks.

There is nothing quite as dangerous as a wounded animal. And if cornered—look out!!

If you are dealing with an ex-spouse who is extremely troublesome, chances are she, like me, has wounds that haven't been healed. A stepmom can't heal, fix, or rescue her from those issues. It helps to know that when a wounded person doesn't take the necessary steps to heal, they inflict their pain on those who come in contact with them. This includes children.

Often it is not intentional, it's just that hurt people, hurt people. And they haven't discovered where freedom can be found. My journey took me to the feet of Christ, where he revealed how to lay down the pain, sorrow, grief, and disgrace. He forgave me of my own sins and taught me how to forgive those who had sinned against me. When emotional liberation finally came, it was as if a huge rock had been lifted off my life. For the first time, I was free. I could breathe.

Occasionally I slip into old destructive patterns. However, the seasons are short-lived. Once God has freed you from the captivity that fear and shame bring, you run to him and fight off the chains of slavery when they attempt to capture and destroy you again.

Tip #39 Provide Stability in the Home

I believe one of the greatest gifts I have given my stepfamily is a glimpse of unity, peace, and stability. After twenty-eight years of being married to their dad, my stepsons and their families have watched how we resolve conflict, weather the storms of life, and grow older together. They have observed how we unite and support each other when life throws us a curve such as illness, death in the family, financial challenges, or job loss. They know we take our vows seriously, and even when we have a fight, they see us return to love.

Gayla Grace, founder of Step Parenting with Grace, says it this way:

> The biggest challenges my husband and I have faced while forming a stepfamily are the favoritism battles between the two sets of children. Although it's natural to have a bias toward your own biological children, we had to repeatedly remind each other that we are all on the same team. This helped us to avoid becoming disconnected over "yours and mine."

Our goal is a legacy of stability founded on faith in Christ. Steve and I provided a home that aimed for harmony and provided tools for effective conflict resolution. This taught my stepsons how to be good husbands and fathers in their own families, and it created an environment filled with laughter instead of chaos and uncertainty.

We weren't perfect, but compassion and commitment were our goals.

Do your stepkids feel safe and loved when they visit? Is your home filled with calm and clear boundaries or tension, confusion, and fighting? Do they hear you or your husband say negative things about their mom that cause knots in their stomachs?

You can only control your part. Therefore, pray for ways to make your home a haven of stability, security, and tranquility where conflict resolution is done with respect.

∽०∾

Lord, I confess that there are days when I border on hating my husband's former spouse. It's embarrassing to admit— but it's true. Honestly, sometimes I truly have no desire to be kind to her. But I also don't want to live my life in bitterness, resentment, and continuous anger.

Jesus, you know what it feels like to be hated, treated like trash, and rejected. And yet you never retaliated. I want to live like that. Teach me how to forgive so that I may be set free. When his ex-wife does something to hurt me, my husband, my children, or my stepchildren, I need your divine wisdom on how to respond.

You are my strength. Help me to see my husband's ex-wife through your compassionate eyes instead of my own resentful perspective. Show me how to promote peace between our homes rather than antagonize. Help me to accept that I cannot control the actions of another individual. I must learn to remain a lady and respond with tact and grace rather than stooping to the level of childish, immature retaliation. I need to remember that my actions are speaking volumes to my children and my stepchildren about how to react when they encounter a person who is determined to hurt them. Let my life be an example of how to cope with difficult people so they leave this house equipped to face conflict.

On my own I do not have the desire, strength, or knowledge on how to live above the circumstances and to cope with a former spouse who desires to hurt me. But you do, Lord. And you will teach me if I sincerely ask.

Suggested Bible verses:
Proverbs 16:32; Isaiah 26:3; Ecclesiastes 7:9; Romans 8:32

4

The Full-Time Stepmom—
When Mom Is Missing

Sometimes I feel like a motherless child.
— Negro spiritual

I will not leave you as orphans.
— Jesus Christ

For a variety of reasons the number of full-time stepmoms has significantly increased over the years. The most common are that the biological mom is:

- Coping with a mental illness and unable to care for a child
- Battling an addiction, perhaps moving in and out of rehabilitation
- Chasing her dreams and trying to "find herself"

- Choosing life with someone she perceives as a soul mate instead of her children
- Living with a physical illness that prevents her from parenting
- Deceased

Life as a full-time stepmom can seem like a maze of benefits and vulnerabilities.

A stepchild, especially if young, may quickly embrace a stepmom. However, that doesn't mean the child isn't still longing and hoping for Mom to return. Parents and children share a unique, unexplainable bond. Keeping this attachment in mind will help when or if the child appears standoffish, depressed, or miserable. As a full-time stepmom, if you brought children into the marriage and they have visitation with their biological dad, it's very possible that you will spend more time with your stepchildren than your own.

Full-time stepmom Heather Hetchler, explains,

> One of the most difficult realities for me when I became a full-time stepmom was that I no longer had time alone with my own children. It was a loss that I had to grieve. I recognized that I must carve out time for my children, even if that means taking a walk together or running errands without the rest of the family. They need one-on-one time with me, and I no longer feel guilty about it.

Tip #40 There Will Be Grief

"I'm embarrassed to admit this, but I have a hard time enjoying myself with my stepkids when my own children are visiting their father. I feel guilty if we go to fun places without them, and I fear that the stepkids will taunt and tease my kids when they return back to our house," stepmom Tiffany admits.

"There is a great deal of sibling rivalry between the two sets of children," she continued. "My stepkids have a deep wound because they have been abandoned by their own mother. Therefore, they like to brag about what we did together while my kids are away. At one point my youngest stepdaughter said to my child, 'Your mom is my mom now and not yours. She has my last name and not your last name so that proves it.' I wanted to choke her."

When a child loses a mother, especially due to desertion, the effects are long-term and devastating. I highly recommend receiving professional help from a therapist who understands. For the full-time stepmom it will take a great deal of hard work to balance the compassion and patience necessary as this child heals, while at the same time protecting her own children from being bullied or mistreated. Tiffany's stepdaughter is obviously attempting to soothe her own abandonment issues by inflicting pain and vengeance on the child who does have a loving mother. This is normal, but should not be ignored.

Reading books and attending workshops regarding children and loss can provide a stepmom with great information about how children cope when a parent is gone. Even if only half the content pertains to her situation, she will obtain insight and skills on how to help the child. Often, these resources offer practical steps to take while helping the child grieve. They also provide suggestions on what to look for in a professional counselor should one be needed.

One of my favorite resources is an older book by Dr. Archibald Hart, *Helping Children Survive Divorce*. He provides excellent insights such as, "Common as divorce is in our society now, few children are really prepared for it when it happens. They expect it to happen to their friends, not to them. About 80 percent of children receive no warning that a divorce is about to take place."[1] Dr. Hart also provides information on subjects such as gender differences, age variation, avoiding common mistakes, how to detect anxiety and depression, and ways to improve the child's self-esteem.

Tip #41 Guard Your Heart

"I was completely devastated when my teen stepdaughter, whom I raised since she was four years old, chose to leave our home and move in with her unstable mother. I walked around the house sobbing for weeks afterward," stepmom Kerry explained.

It's important for a stepmom to prepare for potential pain. If the mother is still alive, it is possible that she may choose to reenter the child's life at some point. This is much more common than most full-time stepmoms realize. And they are ambushed by the sense of loss and betrayal that can accompany her. This mom might stay away for a few years and then reappear, desiring to reestablish a relationship with her child. Begin now to think through how you will handle the anger, frustration, and fear that will automatically arise should this situation occur. Be aware that after the mother appears, the child may reject a stepmom. A child who fears that a good relationship with a stepparent will displease or anger her mom may drop you in order to gain her approval.

Tip #42 Don't Guard Your Heart

This may seem like a contradiction, but hang with me. If you're not careful, preparing for loss can easily turn into a hardened heart. As you consider the potential rejection from your stepchild in favor of the mother, it's important not to erect a thick wall around your heart. In other words, refrain from emotional withdrawal from the child. You should understand the mom's motives and prepare for the problems her return may produce without living in fear or detachment.

This is an extremely sensitive and fragile place for a stepmom to reside emotionally. It will require comfort from your husband

and a few terrific girlfriends. For the full-time stepmom, a strong, encouraging stepmom support group is crucial. They become a lifeline.

Tip #43 The Kids Want Dad

"My husband and I took his daughter to the park. Even though I'm the one who is with her all day, she kept looking to make sure her daddy was watching. I felt hurt. Why didn't she look to me for recognition too?" stepmom Maria sobbed.

As the stepmom, you may be the one staying up all night when your stepchild is sick, holding a little head as they puke. And when that same child is thirty and helping a sick child of their own, they may appreciate you for it. But right now all they really want to know is, "Where's Dad?" This stems from the need for reassurance that the remaining parent is present.

This is reality: When Dad praises an A on the report card, attends the dance recital, or watches them on the swing, that's when the child of divorce receives assurance and comfort. Dr. Hart provides insight: "An absent parent creates an exaggerated need for that parent, and the anxiety increases when this need is not met."[2]

But don't lose heart, they do monitor and take note of a stepmom's acts of kindness too. I'm amazed at the little things I did for my stepsons that they remember now as adults. This reveals that children see the efforts a stepmom makes, whether or not we think they do.

Tip #44 It's Not YOU!

Even after months, maybe years, of full-time helping with homework, wiping snotty noses, and attending soccer games, recognize that your stepchild may still have wounds over the loss of Mom. Remember, hurt people hurt people. For a season the stepmom may be an easy target for the arrows of the child's pain. Understand that the Mother Teresa of stepmoms might be rejected by her stepchildren.

This is where recognizing that some hurts, rejections, and betrayals go so deep that only God can heal them. The good news is—you aren't God. The burden of healing everyone isn't your job. That should prompt a sigh of relief.

Tip #45 Comfort the Broken Heart

A painful task for full-time stepmoms is being the one who helps the child grieve. "Why doesn't my mother love me? Why doesn't she want to see me?" are common cries from these hurting, abandoned children. Knowing what to say and how to comfort them can seem daunting if not impossible. One stepmom agonized, "I was crying as hard as my stepdaughter. I could barely talk." Don't feel bad about weeping with your stepchild. It shows you care.

Even if a stepmom isn't fully bonded with her stepchild yet, whispering reassuring words such as "I'm right here and I will not leave" or "I'm always here for you" are ways a stepmom can comfort the heartbroken child.

After twenty-eight years as a stepmom, I now have grand-children through my stepsons. Whenever the opportunity arises, I like to whisper in their ears, "Nana loves you." I want them to know that they cannot lose—or out-sin—my love. I might be frustrated, hurt, angry, or disappointed with them, but that will not change my love. Communicating unconditional love is one of the ways a full-time stepmom can help her stepchild to become secure in knowing and believing "I am loved, and I am not alone."

Tip #46 Carve Out Couple Time

"As a full-time stepmom I still get a little jealous when other stepmoms say, 'We have all the kids on the same schedule. That way my husband and I have a weekend for just the two of us,'" stepmom Hannah described. "Sometimes I want my husband all to myself. Because my stepchildren are with us 24/7, we had to get creative and ask extended family, friends, or other stepfamily couples to watch my husband's kids occasionally."

When a stepmom never receives a break from her stepkids, it can lead to marital problems. Therefore, it's crucial to set up date nights and special times to reconnect as husband and wife.

Tip #47 Pray

This tip might sound so mundane that you skip it. Please don't.

Sometimes we need a reminder that our humble prayers can change lives. I love this quote by Samuel Chadwick: "The one concern of the devil is to keep Christians from praying. He fears nothing from prayerless studies, prayerless work, and prayerless religion. He laughs at our toil, mocks at our wisdom, but trembles when we pray."[3]

A praying stepmom is a powerful force. Avoid letting resentment, aggravation, dread, or a lack of change cause you to refrain from lifting your cries to heaven. The Holy Father can be trusted with stepfamily complexities and sorrow.

God promises to see, hear, and answer. It's all in his ways and his timing.

～○～

Heavenly Father, calm my anxious heart. I have no idea how to fill the void that this child's mother has left. I am in so far over my head that without your help I could mess this up badly. A fragile, precious life is looking to me for love and validation. I feel so inadequate. And I'm so angry at the birth mom for wounding this beautiful child. But I have been called to this task and my deepest desire is to help this child heal, grow, and become a productive, loving person in today's society.

Holy Spirit, your words reveal that I am unconditionally loved and cherished. This gives me the ability and strength to offer that same compassion and love to my stepchild. You also provide the assurance that you will never leave me. I long to help my stepchild know this truth and to ease any fears of abandonment that were created when the mother disappeared.

My husband and I need you to teach us how to parent. Give us wisdom and insight into what occurs when a child has been abandoned by a mother. Help us to recognize any warning signs that we might require professional help. Place before us resources, support groups, or a counselor if that is needed. Reveal when our schedule is getting so hectic that it is destroying our priorities. Thank you for loving this child more than my husband or I ever could. Thank you for providing everything I will need to be a godly, emotionally stable, and loving stepmom.

Suggested Bible verses:
Psalm 27:10; John 14:18; Matthew 18:14; 1 Corinthians 2:9

5

Things I Wish My Stepmom Knew: A Different Perspective

Two little lines I heard one day, traveling along life's busy way; bringing conviction to my heart, and from my mind would not depart; *only one life, 'twill soon be past, only what's done for Christ will last.*

—C. T. Studd, missionary
to China 1860–1931

"I have seen the Lord!"

—Mary of Magdala, formerly
possessed by seven demons and the
first person to see the risen Christ

A few years ago I was asked to speak to stepmoms at an international MOPS (Mothers of Preschoolers) conference. Around twenty ladies joined the gathering as I shared how to become a smart stepmom, and they loved it.

What happened after the session is the interesting part. Sitting at my book table in the large convention hall I noticed a pattern emerge that I had not yet experienced.

Young woman after young woman would walk by my table, glance at my book *The Smart Stepmom,* and walk by with a "that doesn't apply to me" look on her face. A few steps away they would stop, turn around, and come back. Each one would pick up a copy and look through the chapters, often with tears welling. I engaged them in conversation, explaining the book contents as I always do, and without fail they responded with almost identical phrases. "I am not a stepmom, but I have one. My dad remarried __ years ago. I'd love to buy her this book, but I'm sure she would be offended."

I would take each woman's hand and reply, "I've had two stepmoms—I understand." Knowing I understood, they continued with their stories. Soon it dawned on me; I was missing a prime opportunity to hear their perspective. As the day wore on I began to ask, "If you could tell your stepmom anything, without fear that she or your dad would get mad at you, what would it be?"

The following tips are based on comments from adult, teen, and young stepkids.

Tip #48 "It Feels Like I Lost My Dad"

Without a doubt, hands down, no competition, the number one response from stepkids—young and old—is that they feel like they lost their dad when he got remarried. This may actually be true or it might be a perception. Regardless, a stepmom can go a long way to alleviate the issue by encouraging her husband to spend time alone with his kids and grandkids. It's as simple as that.

Tip #49 "I Like You"

Stepmoms often bring warmth, stability, cleanliness, organization, clean laundry, and home-cooked meals back into the house. Therefore, the kids like having her there. They also sense that she really cares about them. Several stepkids shared with me, "My stepmom is one of the nicest, kindest, most loving people I have ever met. I'm so glad to have her in my life."

Ann, a stepmom friend, shared with me a note she received from her teen stepson. He was working on a school paper and shared his comments with her. A childless stepmom and an ordained minister, she wasn't sure she was having much of an impact in her role as a stepmom. However, his words confirm that when it comes to parenting, more is caught than taught: "My stepmother, Ann, vibrantly exemplifies the love of Jesus. Even on the toughest days in her corporate job, I see her look to God for comfort and clarity. Her love of God has been an example and an inspiration for me on my spiritual journey. While she's not a perfect person, she looks toward biblical standards for everything. Her whole life is about her Creator. She lives a life of worship, not just in church on Sunday. When I am in a room with her I notice her unique spirit and realize she's been changed by the one true God. She's prepared me for living without relying solely on my parents, but on God. I'm learning to let go and let God control my life."

I've got one thing to say, "Way to go, Stepmom Ann!"

Tip #50 "My Mom Hates You"

Stepkids wish their stepmom understood why they are in conflict and turmoil about how to respond to her. They want her to know that they don't view her as a bad person, and given different circumstances they would enjoy her company. If the stepmom is hated by the mother, the children's loyalty will remain with their mom almost every time. They will withhold their love for a stepmom in order to keep peace and allegiance to the biological parent.

Tip #51 "I Don't Like Sharing My Dad With Your Kids/Grandkids"

"My father has his own grandkids. Why does he have to spend so much time with and dote on hers?" a thirty-something woman stated.

Daughters in particular get really angry when they feel as though a stepmom has caused their dad to withdraw his attention and affection from his biological kids and shifted it toward the stepmother's family.

To take this one level higher, if she feels her own children are being slighted and losing Grandpa, and the stepmom is replacing his grandkids with her own—look out!! It can get ugly.

Because the woman in the home usually manages the calendar and we naturally gravitate to our own families, it's very easy for a stepmom and her husband to spend more time with her family than with his. This is especially true if the stepmom feels uncomfortable or slighted around his kids.

It's possible that the dad doesn't even realize they are spending more time with her family than with his. However, a smart stepmom doesn't try to replace her husband's kids with her family. She recognizes that it will only widen the gap and the dissention between her and her stepkids.

Tip #52 "Thanks for Making My Dad Happy Again"

"My father was so sad after my mom died. It's wonderful to see him laugh again," stepdaughter Crystal shared with me.

"She has been a godsend to him and to us. Now I don't worry about him being alone."

Even kids who have lived through the divorce of their parents may observe how the stepmom has brought joy back into their dad's life. If their dad was extremely lonely after a divorce, and the kids felt they had to take care of him or provide ways to help him overcome the grief, they might feel relieved.

"After the divorce I was worried my dad might take his life," stepson Ted explained. "Since he met Noreen, he's back to himself. I'm so grateful to her for helping my dad enjoy living again."

Tip #53 "Why Do You Dislike Me?"

People—including kids—can tell when you don't like them. And it's very easy for a stepmom to dislike her stepkids. Let's face it; whether big or small, they are sometimes self-centered, mouthy, menacing, and hurtful intrusions to life. During my stepmom journey there were times I struggled to embrace my husband's kids.

Then I would remember my vow. When I stood before God and made a lifelong commitment to my husband, I promised to walk alongside all of him—including his kids. And I knew if I was willing, God would teach me how to love people that hurt me, including my stepsons.

I can't make my stepsons love or even like me, but I can show them that I care. A driving force was that I wanted them to feel loved and secure in our home. I know how hard it is when parents divorce and you feel like you don't belong anywhere. I didn't want my stepsons to feel that way.

Therefore, I made a conscious decision to show them "I may not always like your choices, but I will always care about you." When they were younger, it meant making some of the foods they like and attending basketball games. When they entered their twenties, this morphed into alleviating stepfamily wedding stress and embracing their new wives. And now that they are dads, I show my affection by loving their children.

It's a choice and it takes time. I haven't always done it perfectly. I'm certain my occasional bad attitude was revealed by my body language. But I've worked hard to communicate that I care and have compassion toward them.

Tip #54 "Thanks for Reaching Out to Me"

One of the things a smart stepmom understands is that she may not see the fruit from her labor until the kids become adults.

"When I joined the military, that's when I realized what a great stepmom I have," Michael explained. "Boot camp was a time to reflect on what is important in life. And I remembered all the times when I was younger that my stepmom made special meals for me and helped me with my homework. She taught me to be respectful to others too. I'm glad she is in my life."

"Plus," he added, "She sends me stuff from home that I love and I can't get now. She's great."

My friend Carrie Soares is one smart stepmom. She grew up in a stepfamily and is using that difficult experience to mold her decisions and actions as a stepmom. She accepts her unique role and why it is crucial to learn, recognize, and admit when she is doing something wrong.

She has given me permission to share the insights and encouragement she offers to her fellow stepmoms:

The position you hold in your stepchild's life is extremely influential even when he or she doesn't act like it. You will deeply hurt your stepchild, and the future of your relationship, if you criticize their mother or make the child feel like a visitor in your home. Remember, the child was there first. Even if their parents' marriage was extremely unhealthy, there is still a small place in the child's heart that wishes it could and would have worked out. Give your stepchild permission to grieve the loss of the original family.

As a stepmom you have the unique opportunity to know your stepchild from an objective point of view. If trust is built, the child may reveal problems or situations with a stepparent that they might not divulge to a biological parent.

On behalf of stepchildren everywhere, thank you for each and every time you've chosen to engage when you didn't want to and shared your advice, money, french fries, skills, car, home, and time with your stepchild.

As a stepchild myself, I say thank you for the times you helped your stepchild learn how to read, tie their shoes, brush their teeth, drive, cook, put makeup on, pray, and balance a checkbook. Thank you for the times you avoided saying something critical about the mom, dad, or child.

Now you know why I view my friend Carrie as one smart stepmom.

Tip #55 "My Dad Is Acting Like a Teenager. It's Ridiculous."

When we enter a new romantic relationship we often act like—um, how can I say this nicely—fools! The person may be giddy and talk incessantly about their new love. They flit around on a perpetual cloud. It's lovely—for the person in love. For those observing the behavior, it seems ridiculous.

Add the stepfamily dynamic, and you have a more complicated yuck factor to consider. In general, kids are uncomfortable thinking about their parents from a sexual perspective. And when they witness affection between a parent and stepparent, it triggers troubling thoughts and emotions. To be blunt—the kids think it's gross and disturbing. They don't like it. "Why are you kissing my mom? It doesn't feel right."

This is another form of grief for the child (including adult children). It is a reminder that the former marriage is over, particularly if the mom and dad didn't show affection toward each other in the marriage. If children have never seen their dad hug or kiss another woman, this may be extremely awkward.

During the dating season it's advisable to keep physical contact between the couple to a minimum, gradually adding holding hands, etc. After the marriage it's best to observe how they react when their dad shows affection toward the stepmom, and decide whether a discussion should take place.

For the stepmom, it's advisable to refrain from ignoring the child's reaction or having an "it's too bad if you don't like it" attitude. That doesn't mean the couple needs to avoid any physical contact in front of the kids. Merely take it slow if the kids reveal resistance.

One suggestion is to set up a code word that alerts the couple when the child is feeling uncomfortable. That way when the stepchild speaks the code word, everyone can laugh, and it lightens the atmosphere.

Tip #56 "I Can Tell You Things I Can't Tell My Parents"

One of the perks of being a stepmom is that the kids often view you as a confidante or an ally. In my senior year of high school I told my stepdad about my dad's wife being pregnant. I wouldn't tell my mom because I knew she would be furious. (He agreed.) It was "our secret" until my mom found out from a family member a few years later. By that time I was older and it didn't matter as much.

Sometimes a stepchild will share day-to-day school events; other times it's much more serious. "My ten-year-old stepdaughter told me that she feels uncomfortable around her mom's new boyfriend. She doesn't like the way he looks at her, plus he gives her long hugs," stepmom Sabrina expressed. "She fears her mother or father might be mad at her if she tells anyone. Although I hate being in the middle of this awkward situation, I'm so glad she trusts me. After his daughter left I spoke with my husband. We are coming up with a plan together."

In this ever-changing world, kids need an ally more than ever. And sometimes that person is the stepmom.

Tip #57 "Are You Getting My Inheritance?"

A common resentment that arises with adult stepkids is the issue of money or an inheritance. They often wonder if the stepmom is going to receive their dad's life insurance, bank account, property, and investments when he dies.

It is vitally important for the stepfamily couple to discuss this situation, preferably before they marry. Each person needs to clearly explain and listen to what the other views as reasonable. If they strongly disagree and cannot resolve the issue, it is an indication that they should not marry.

Once in agreement on how they will handle their financial future, it's crucial for them to obtain an attorney and draw up the paperwork in a will or a trust. This person should be someone who can ask the hard questions that will force the couple to review numerous end-of-life decisions. This includes financial and property resolutions, but also sensitive issues such as who is in charge of making the choices regarding a feeding tube or life support.

If that wasn't complicated enough, there is one more vital step. Your husband needs to be the one to share these decisions with his children. It is not the stepmom's role, and it can create further complexities if she steps in. It's an extremely selfish man who leaves these issues behind after he dies, which forces his grieving, fragile wife and kids to "duke it out" after he is gone.

Tip #58 "I Feel Terrible for the Way I've Treated You"

I once read this quote by David Brinkley: "A successful woman is one who can lay a firm foundation with the bricks others have thrown at her."

Over the last twenty years, my adult stepsons, sometimes via their wives, have each made comments about how badly they treated me when they were growing up. We laugh about it now, and I even call myself the "wicked stepmother" in front of them.

My stepsons know that I had two stepmoms while growing up, so I understand. However, it is nice to hear a stepchild admit that they were a bit of a brat. This usually occurs after they have children of their own and they recognize how hard it is to be a parent. My oldest stepson even has a stepdaughter now.

That's when a stepmom chuckles.

Listen to the words one stepmom received after a few years of battling with a difficult teen stepdaughter:

I wouldn't be the person I am today if my dad hadn't introduced me to you. There was a night a few years ago when we were having a family meeting and I said you weren't my parent. There isn't a day that goes by that I don't think about saying those hurtful words to you. I do see you as a parent and not just a stepmom but as my best friend too. For some time I have thought about apologizing to you but I didn't know how. I can't wait to spend the next four years waking up seeing your pre-shower face, while at the same time my alarm is blasting for fifteen minutes. Most of all I can't wait to start the journey with you, my dad, me, my brother, and the new baby.

Not every stepmom will receive a letter like this, but many will. The tip is to keep doing the right thing one step after the other. And leave the rest up to the One greater than ourselves.

∽∘∾

Gracious God, fill my heart with your exuberant gift of love. Teach me to be sensitive, compassionate, and teachable regarding my stepchildren. Help me to listen to their actions as well as their words so that I may know their true needs. Reveal to me their hopes and fears, and then convey how I can do practical things that will minister to those issues.

Lord, I need to know when it is wise to be vulnerable with my stepchildren and when it is preferable to guard my heart. Provide me with an awareness of how to communicate your love to them so that they know there is a Creator who will never leave them and who longs to set them free from fears and discouragement. Thank you for your unwavering faithfulness and compassion.

Suggested Bible verses:
1 John 4:10; Psalm 16:7–8; Isaiah 40:28

6

The Childless and Child-Free Stepmom—Unique Challenges

A woman is like a tea bag—you can't tell how strong she is until you put her in hot water.

—Eleanor Roosevelt

Give all your worries and cares to God, for he cares about you.

—Simon Peter, fisherman, denied knowing Christ, praised by Jesus as "the Rock"

E very pre-marriage couple should discuss whether or not they desire to have children. However, for the stepfamily couple it is even more important. Adding an "ours" baby to the stepfamily mix has numerous pros and cons. (*The Smart Stepmom* offers an entire chapter on the subject.)

There is a big difference between being childless and child free. The woman who is childless has no biological children of her own, but she desires to be a mother. A child-free woman is one who is childless by choice.

A stepmom in either of these categories faces unique challenges. First, let's look at the childless stepmom.

The Childless Stepmom

It is not uncommon for a woman who has never had a child to become a stepmom later in life. This makes the decision whether to add a baby a bit more complicated. Infertility is also not uncommon among stepmoms. Therefore, it is vitally important for the couple to discuss the level of importance of adding an "ours" baby. Typically, hubby is okay with the decision either way. He may not have a desire to have another child, but he is willing if his wife feels strongly about it.

Tip #59 When Your Husband Believes You Already Have Kids

"My husband doesn't grasp why I want to have a child," stepmom Marianne shared. "He keeps insisting that I already have three kids and asking why I need more. But I don't have three kids—he does!" she continued. "Why doesn't he understand that I want a child of my own? If I try to explain, he becomes angry and says if I really loved his kids they would be enough."

This is a serious marital situation.

This scenario stems from a husband having an expectation that his children will meet his wife's maternal desires. He views it as a personal attack, and his wife as being unreasonable, if she craves a child of her own.

The root of the problem is a distorted view of stepfamily formation. The hubby so desperately wants to live as a first-time family, as opposed to a stepfamily, that he ignores or denies that a stepparent loves a stepchild differently. The disappointment and anger he expresses toward his second wife prevents him from understanding why the stepmom doesn't view his children as hers. The reason is quite simple.

They aren't her kids.

Many women have a yearning to become pregnant, feel a baby grow in the womb, and give birth. It's the way they are wired. And it frequently has nothing to do with how a stepmom feels about or the relationship she has with her stepchildren. It is merely a female desire.

When a woman believes her spouse is refusing to hear her feminine heartbeat, or he is unwilling to have compassion toward her maternal longing, it can be the catalyst for marital disaster. Counseling or life coaching is often necessary to resolve this issue.

Tip #60 Coping With Infertility

If a stepmom has married later in life, it increases the possibility that the couple will not be able to have a child of their own. Many stepfamily couples in this circumstance choose fertility treatments. In vitro fertilization can take several attempts before it is successful, and it is often very expensive. Health insurance rarely covers the procedures. If another child is more important to the wife than to the husband, it can create tension for the couple. Therefore, it's extremely important for them to decide whether they have the financial resources, time, and patience for fertility treatments. It's best to have a discussion regarding their moral perspectives, the length of time they will commit, and the dollar amount they are willing to spend on infertility treatments. This helps to prevent conflict and disappointment later on.

Tip #61 When Adoption Is an Option

"We tried for a short time to have a baby, but I'm forty-three and it's just not going to happen. We began looking into adoption and both of us are excited," stepmom Veronica shares. "Fortunately, I have a few friends who have already adopted a child. They are giving me excellent advice on domestic and foreign adoption."

To avoid unexpected surprises or disappointments, it's advisable to consult an attorney who specializes in adoption before pursuing this option. Each state has different adoption policies and laws.

Tip #62 When Your Husband Changes His Mind

One of the worst situations is when a husband tells his wife he is willing to have more children, and then after the wedding he changes his mind. "I feel deceived," stepmom Brenda tearfully explains. "He knew how badly I wanted a baby of my own. I made this very clear before we got married. And now he says that the stepfamily stress is too much and he doesn't want to add another child. What am I supposed to do with the longing I have to be a mother?"

If this couple doesn't come to a mutual agreement, the marriage is in jeopardy because the mandatory trust factor is evaporating. I understand how a father might think the stepfamily situation would be easier than it actually is, but that doesn't negate the promise he made to his wife before they got married.

To complicate the issue, if Brenda's friends and family are naïve about the complexities of stepfamily living and the radical difference between first and second marriages, they may be causing more tension. Women who don't understand stepfamilies can be extremely vicious and judgmental toward a stepmom who doesn't view her husband's children as her own.

This couple needs therapy immediately.

Tip #63 Should We Consider the Kids?

Should a couple consult the kids from the previous marriage(s) before adding more children to the stepfamily? Typically my answer is yes. But they should not be allowed to dictate the decision. Find an opportune time and gather the whole family together so that the dad can pose the question, "What would you think if we had a baby?" Don't be surprised if the answers vary depending on the age and gender of the child. Initially younger children will likely be excited about the idea; teenagers often reject the suggestion.

Factors that make it more likely that adding a new baby to the mix will have a positive impact include:

- Overall stability, peace, and effective co-parenting between the two homes
- Children who have a good relationship with a stepparent, and generally view her as a positive influence on their lives
- Children who are in their dad's home full-time or spend a significant amount of time with the stepmom

Factors that decrease the chance that adding a new baby will result in a smooth transition are:

- Stress, fighting, and tension between the two homes
- Children who are resentful or angry about having a stepmom
- Children who view the stepfamily as the reason why the marriage between their mom and dad ended
- A dad who is disengaged or spends very little time with his children from the first marriage
- Children who live a long distance away from their dad and see him infrequently
- A former spouse who tells the children that a new baby will replace them in their dad's life

I strongly suggest the stepfamily couple spend a great deal of time discussing the matter and obtaining insight from a third party who understands stepfamily dynamics before making the decision to add a child. This can help the couple prepare for any positives or negatives that may arise when a new baby is added.

The Child-Free Stepmom

At fifteen years of age I knew that I didn't want to bring a child into this world. I joined a handful of women who are "childless by choice." Until recently I didn't share that information with many women because often they think it's extremely odd. As I age I'm more concerned about helping others heal than I am about what people think of me. I have stepped out on a limb and share why I don't have children.

The lack of children isn't normally what triggers pain for the child-free stepmom, it's the comments from those who don't understand. "I grew up in a very abusive, neglectful home. By the time I was thirteen I knew I never wanted to have children," Leslie explained. "I didn't want to bring another person into this hurting world. I couldn't take that risk. Most women assume I don't have kids because I'm self-centered or that I wanted a lofty career, but that's totally untrue." She proceeded, "It's not that I didn't want children. I actually think I would have been a great mom. People typically don't understand my perspective, so I rarely share. My choice was to put aside what I wanted for what I felt was best."

Leslie's thoughts parallel my own. Whether you agree or disagree with the decision not to have children, it's important to understand that you might not know all the reasons why a woman is child free. It's important to refrain from speaking words that inflict needless pain.

Tip #64 Ignore Judgmental Attitudes

One of the things child-free stepmoms face is judgment from women who have chosen to have a child or those who desire to have a child. I'm often treated as an outsider merely because I have never carried a child in my womb. However, I know a great deal about the needs of children.

When my former sister-in-law chose to leave her marriage to my brother, he raised their two little girls, ages two and six, as a single dad. I lived around the corner from him, and to this day I love those two girls as if they were my own. They are adults now with kids of their own, but that doesn't change my overwhelming affection for them. I believe one of the reasons I didn't have children was to help fill the void left by their mother when she walked out.

There will always be women who criticize and do not understand the child-free stepmom. Let it go and surround yourself with those who desire to encourage and support you.

Tip #65 Instant Motherhood: A Culture Shock

A child-free stepmom may have a bigger adjustment to the sudden daily duties of being a mother when she marries a man with kids.

"I was unprepared for how much of my time would be absorbed in being a stepmom," Stephanie said. "Before the marriage I was used to coming and going around the needs of my own schedule. But now I have to check the calendar constantly to evaluate visitation times, sporting events, school commitments, pickup and drop-off times, and a plethora of other things which now invade my schedule. I care about my stepkids, and I'm willing to learn how to cope. However, it's been a huge adjustment."

Tip #66 Overcoming Guilt and Shame

"I truly miss my 'me' time. I spent most of my adult life doing the things I wanted to do. Going to work, getting to the gym, taking my dog out for a walk, and running errands were the only things I really had on my agenda. Now I don't have a spare minute to get my hair cut. My life is constantly filled with tasks for my husband, his kids, my in-laws, and other people. I'm starting to resent it."

It's important for a stepmom to carve out time to do the things she used to do before she became a wife and mother. This is why girlfriends are vitally important to stepfamily sanity. Certainly life will never be exactly as it was before the marriage, and that's a good thing. But that doesn't mean that a stepmom must deny herself time to rejuvenate and refresh.

Even Jesus saw the value in alone time. "The apostles gathered around Jesus. They told him all they had done and taught. But many people were coming and going. So they did not even have a chance to eat. Then Jesus said to his apostles, 'Come with me by yourselves to a quiet place. You need to get some rest.' So they went away by themselves in a boat to a quiet place" (Mark 6:30–32).

If the Son of God and his disciples needed a break from the constant demands and needs of others, then why do we feel ashamed when we require the same respite? I'm not suggesting that we become self-centered and ignore the needs of others, I'm merely saying it's okay to rest and do something fun.

Tip #67 Answering "Mommy" Questions

In preparation for attending a bridal or baby shower or any other occasion where the discussion is likely to focus on the joys of motherhood, it might be a good idea to prepare beforehand.

This is where a stepmom is often barraged by numerous questions such as, "When are you going to have a baby?" "How many children do you have?" or "Where is your little bundle of joy?" I have some standard default answers. The most common being "Steve has two children from his first marriage." If I determine that this is not going to satisfy the curiosity, I then smile sweetly and add, "They were eleven and thirteen when we married, and adolescents will kill any maternal instincts." Everyone usually laughs, and so do I. This typically shuts down the conversation—which is my goal. It's a polite way of saying, "It's none of your business."

Whether childless or child free, a stepmom should not be ashamed, embarrassed, or intimidated by the fact that she does not have her own biological child. All women can be tremendous, loving, and effective stepmoms who play a significant role and are a powerful positive influence in the life of a stepchild.

∽၀ဢ

Heavenly Father, my husband and I desperately need your wisdom. Bringing another child into the world is a big decision, and we seek your guidance. If adoption is your direction for us, please bring the child that you have designed to complete our family.

Help me, Lord, to be sensitive to the needs of my husband and his children, and yet not ignore the desires of my own heart. You alone know my innermost being. You created me. You know everything about me, and I do not need to be afraid.

Teach me to let go of the things I cannot control, and to remember that you love me and my stepfamily more than I could ever imagine.

Suggested Bible verse:
Psalm 139

93

7

"What Did You Say?" Educating Family and Friends

I've learned that people will forget what you said, people will forget what you did, but people will never forget how you made them feel.

—Maya Angelou

Whatever is true, whatever is noble, whatever is right, whatever is pure, whatever is lovely, whatever is admirable—if anything is excellent or praiseworthy—think about such things.

—Paul of Tarsus, Jewish leader who murdered Christians

I was the only stepmom attending the event, but that didn't prevent me from immediately warming up to the other moms in the group. They were various ages, in many different stages of life, and had a wide range of experiences. Over the weekend several of them shared how stressful it is to raise children in today's world.

Their openness and humility provided a safe place to share the complications of being a stepmom. Several of them replied, "I had no idea that stepmoms faced those situations." But a few moms disliked my insights, and one criticized me.

She and I agreed to disagree. But I was wounded by her sharp words and judgment. I wept during the drive home, thinking, "Maybe she is right, maybe I'm too negative. Maybe I don't know what I'm talking about."

The following weekend I was leading a stepmom event. As I began speaking I observed the ladies seated before me nodding and smiling as I spoke. Their faces communicated, "Finally! Someone understands my life."

At the end of the event one woman with tear-filled eyes introduced herself saying, "Your stepmom book saved my life and my marriage. No one else understands. I don't know how to say thank you." In that moment I realized that when a person has never experienced life in a stepfamily, they do not comprehend the vast complexities in the stepfamily structure, the difficulties of parenting between two homes, and the time it takes for the newly formed family to bond.

It was my job to conquer my insecurities. I had to learn a better way to respond when wounding words came my way.

When people make foolish comments, it's often out of ignorance. Sometimes a person assumes they understand stepfamily living because they read an article or a stepfamily lives next door. For this person a great comeback can be, "Before I got married I thought I understood stepfamily living. Boy!! It was a huge wake-up call when I discovered I knew almost nothing."

Those of us who grew up with a stepmom can add, "I had a stepmom growing up, so I foolishly assumed that taught me how to be a stepmom. I was wrong."

This normally gets the conversation moving into a place where you can explain in more detail should you desire.

Tip #68 Choosing to Love Your Stepkids—A Different Kind of Affection

Nasty comments often come a stepmom's way when some well-meaning person assumes a stepmom should love her husband's kids exactly the same way she does her own. The unrealistic thinking that a stepmom is going to automatically and fervently love a child she barely knows, who often dislikes her, and who came from another woman's body, is ridiculous.

But I've stopped counting the number of stepmoms who write and tell me, "I finally got the courage to be honest and speak what I feel as a stepmom. But then my sister (aunt, mother-in-law, pastor's wife, pick one) said I should be ashamed of myself for saying that I love my own children more than I do my husband's. I feel terrible. I do love my stepkids, and I grow to love them more as time goes by, but I guess it's not enough. I've often wondered if I really am the wicked stepmom. Now I know for sure—this proves it."

And the mantle of shame this woman unnecessarily carries grows heavier with each comment. She eventually tells no one how she really feels, thinking she is the worst stepmom on the planet.

A better response is: "Fortunately I've been educating myself on stepfamilies. And a common thread in each resource is that it's unrealistic for a stepmom to love her husband's kids exactly the same way she loves her own biological children. I work very hard to build a bridge with his kids, and I choose to care deeply about them. A chosen love is still love. Maybe even better, because it takes more work."

Tip #69 You Simply Fell in Love With a Man Who Has Kids

"You must be crazy to take on someone else's kids. I'd never do that," is a recurring expression heard by stepmoms. I understand why it's popular. We live in a self-centered world and walking into a situation that requires a lot of hard work is undesirable.

A way to shut down further discussion is by sharing, "I fell in love with a man with children. I am shocked by the complexities, but my husband is such a great guy that he is worth it. My role as a stepmom is really hard, and I need support. I know you mean well, but I need encouragement, not negativity."

Tip #70 You Can't Fix Stupid

Probably one of the most hurtful statements said to the childless stepmom is "You aren't a real mom. You wouldn't understand." I've watched stepmoms cry a river of tears over this statement. It's the motherhood version of "mean girls." And if I'm sincerely honest, I don't really get why one woman feels the need to emotionally attack and crush another woman. It's beyond me.

I recently read how this cattiness between women is birthed in young girls. Authors Degler and Coughlin share that the relational aggression between girls such as spreading rumors, teasing, threatening to exclude someone, and shunning is used to bully other girls. They add, "Physical punches may not be thrown, but the emotional pain is devastating and, over time, can lead girls and women to believe females, by nature, are untrustworthy, devious, and manipulative—in a word, catty."[1]

The act of emotionally bashing another person in an attempt to feel superior is sad, painful, and unproductive. But there are women who do it all the time.

My suggestion is a simple response: "I may not have given birth to a child, but that doesn't mean I don't play a mom-like role in the lives of my stepkids. I carpool, cook meals, wash laundry, place Band-Aids on their cuts, and help with homework the same way any mom does. I play a significant role in their lives, and I work at doing it well."

Tip #71 You Didn't Know What You Were Getting Into

A person better be ready to duck if she chooses to tell a stepmom, "You knew what you were getting into when you married a man with kids." To a stepmom, "Them is fightin' words!"

Before the wedding most stepmoms are unaware of how challenging the journey will be. They know at the altar they are saying, "I do" to a new merging family. But a new stepmom is usually either in denial or uninformed of how she automatically inherited a whole host of people and things over which she has no control, such as a former spouse, the former spouse's husband (stepdad), the stepdad's family, ex-in-laws, the friends her hubby jointly has with his ex-wife, and grieving kids.

It throws salt into the wound when people assume she should have known all of this beforehand. The truth is we don't know what we don't know. A good response for this comment is "Even though I did read books and attended a stepfamily seminar before the wedding, I could never have imagined or predicted the number of things involved in blending two homes. I had no idea how complicated it would be to keep this marriage alive and thriving. My husband and I have been ambushed by stepfamily complexities, but we are committed to making it work."

Tip #72 Listen to Wise Words

Sometimes the questions or remarks made to a stepmom are from women who genuinely care and desire a deeper understanding of stepfamily life. This comes in the form of statements such as, "Too bad his kids don't live with you full time. It would be so much easier for everyone, including the kids if they didn't have to juggle two homes."

This well-meaning observation appears logical and practical. That's when it's a stepmom's job to kindly educate others on kids and divorce. Explain that the children who do the best after divorce are the ones who have an ongoing relationship with both parents. And although it is hard on everyone to shuffle between two homes, with two different sets of rules and discipline styles, it's crucial for the children to maintain a good, steady relationship with both the mom and dad. This is true even if one parent surpasses the other in parenting.

Usually the conversation is beneficial and instructional, which offers the person who made the comment the opportunity to be educated on the subject of kids and divorce as well as stepfamilies.

Tip #73 Stop Attempting to Explain

I have several girlfriends who long to have children but are unable to conceive. These friendships provide me with a deeper understanding and sensitivity into their world of grief, pain, loss, and frustration. Therefore, I'm taken aback when I meet a woman for the first time and her immediate question to me is "How many children do you have?" It is not a difficult situation for me, but my mind automatically travels to my infertile friends. I think about how this simple and mundane question must stab them in the heart, and the womb, every time it is asked.

That's why, when meeting a new woman, I never bring up children. I stay under the mommy radar as much as possible. If I'm having a conversation with a woman who has children, she will normally bring the subject up eventually. When I am posed the "kid question" I reply, "My husband, Steve, has two children from his first marriage. They are grown now with kids of their own, so we have grandkids." This typically satisfies the curiosity and takes the conversation in another direction.

Some people don't want to know how hard it is being a step-mom. And if they were against your husband's remarriage, they may assume you got what you deserved. In either case it's best to know when to stop trying to explain.

At the women's event I mentioned earlier, I realized that no amount of explaining was going to make my point clear. This woman had made up her mind. She knew more about step-families than I did, even though she has never been in one. She had a preconceived idea that all families are the same. And although a wonderful woman, she wasn't teachable at that moment. Once I realized this fact, I stepped back and changed the subject.

I was still hurt and licking my wounds because I wanted her to understand. Even deeper, I wanted her to like me and to think I'm a good woman. And I walked away feeling she thought less of me as a Christian, a wife, and an author. But I had to shake off the discouragement and pessimism because it's a lie.

Tip #74 Are You Teachable?

It's possible that a friend might say something to a stepmom that she doesn't want to hear. I'm not talking about the people who intentionally make hurtful comments. I'm referring to the true friend who desires our well-being and can see the things that we cannot.

In my own life I have a few women that I trust to tell me the truth about myself. I know they love me; therefore when they speak something into my life that is unpleasant—I listen. That doesn't mean it's easy, or that I don't desire to reject their advice, but deep inside I know they wouldn't say it to me if they didn't view it as important.

Do you have a trusted female friend who can be honest? Can she tell you when you are wrong? Are you willing to listen and consider that she might be right? I've discovered that if I surrender my own preconceived thoughts and become teachable, this type of friendship can enhance my life immensely. It helps to prune off the ugly stuff and dead branches that don't produce anything fruitful or productive in my stepmom journey.

The Bible agrees and calls it iron sharpening iron.[2]

Tip #75 Your Situation Is Unique

Although stepmoms have a lot in common, each stepmom marches to a different drumbeat of life. Her unique background, circumstances, and family setting makes her extraordinary. A stepmom must learn that what works in one stepfamily situation might not work in hers.

There is a priceless treasure in finding a community of positive thinking stepmom sisters. Many times they will be the only way to keep your sanity. Friends and family mean well, but unless they have walked the stepfamily journey they usually won't get it!

When I get discouraged and I feel like I can't do one thing right, that's when it's time to take a moment of silence and solitude. In prayer I choose to leap into my heavenly Father's arms, lay my head against his chest, and hear his heartbeat that rhythmically whispers to this weary child, "Laura, I love you. I'm right here. I'll teach you how to be a smart stepmom. Your methods aren't always perfect, but your heart is right. My love is not based on performance. I love you just because I created you. Lift up your head, Laura, and embrace truth."

When I spend time with Jesus and allow him to whisper words of affirmation, truth, and hope, I can feel the tension, frustration, despair, and anger melt away.

If you desire a deeper understanding of this intimate relationship with God and his Son, Jesus, the last chapter addresses this subject.

Precious Papa, there are some people I really dislike. This is not a surprise; you know everything about me. And yet you tell me to treat each person with dignity regardless of how they behave. On my own strength this is impossible. But with you all things are possible.

Jesus, you know exactly what it feels like to be misunderstood, abused, ridiculed, and ostracized. Teach me how to react when people say hurtful, inconsiderate, or thoughtless comments. Help me to remain a lady even when I desire to retaliate with a nasty zinger.

Whenever possible, help me to educate those who are willing to learn about the complexities of stepfamily living. Provide me with the discernment of when to speak and when to keep silent, and then to leave the results with you.

Suggested Bible verses:
Hebrews 2:18; 4:15–16; Colossians 3:12–15

Mary Had a Little Lamb

Mary had a little Lamb
His grace was white as snow,
Everywhere the holy One went
His love would overflow.

Angels sang to shepherds,
A manger gave Him rest,
He bridged the gap to heaven
So mankind would be blessed.

This little Lamb named Jesus
Cleanses us from sin,
Wise men—then and now
Know the victory He'll win.

And everyone who seeks Him
He calmly lingers near,
And softly keeps on calling,
Until we choose to hear.

Mary had a little Lamb
Who hears His people cry,
He offers us a golden crown
To reign with Him on high!
                —Laura Petherbridge

8

Holidays, Weddings, and Mother's Day—Oh My!

Thanksgiving dinners take eighteen hours to prepare.
They are consumed in twelve minutes. Half-times take
twelve minutes. This is not coincidence.

—Erma Bombeck

My soul glorifies the Lord and my spirit rejoices in God
my Savior. . . . The Mighty One['s] . . . mercy extends
to those who fear him, from generation to generation.

—Mary, God's choice to be the
mother of his Son, Jesus Christ

I can't wait till my stepkids turn eighteen," Vicki shared.
"When they become adults all of this stepfamily drama
will end—won't it?"
I chuckled.

It's true that many of the issues, such as visitation schedules, child support, and helping with homework, will end as the children get older. But that doesn't necessarily mean that stepfamily issues go away. They will likely morph into new kinds of issues. Some situations will be more manageable because you are now dealing with an adult child who can reason and think on their own.

Special occasions tend to be one of the trigger areas where stepfamilies struggle regardless of the age of the children. Here are a few tips.

Holidays

Tip #76 Expect the Unexpected

"My mom refuses to treat my stepchildren the same as her grandchildren," Mason, a dad attending my stepfamily event, lamented. "My wife is hurt and furious, and I don't blame her. I'm caught in the middle between my parents and my spouse. I'm starting to dread the entire holiday season."

After twenty-eight years of stepfamily living, I remember more than one Christmas when I wanted to walk out to the nativity scene in my front yard and ask baby Jesus to move over so I could squeeze into the manger beside him. It didn't matter that I was living in New York, with an icy temperature of ten degrees outside. All I wanted was that "heavenly peace" the Christmas carols were depicting.

The various traditions and visitation schedules in the multiple homes, multiple parents, multiple grandparents, and multiple in-laws of stepfamily living often produce tension during the season of good cheer. Therefore, to maintain sanity it's wise to expect new and unusual issues to arise during the holidays. Each family will have a learning curve on what, when, and how to prepare for the festivities. The stepfamily that expects the unexpected will handle the issues much better than one that is ambushed.

Tip #77 Murder Norman Rockwell

Most stepmoms desire to create a warm, loving home during the holidays. And that's a good thing. However, like many other women, we can drive ourselves crazy attempting to make it perfect. Blame Norman Rockwell for the unrealistic images of what the dinner table should look like during a holiday feast. If Norman had grown up in a stepfamily, he likely would have depicted the scene with an empty chair or two at the table. After a remarriage children are shuffled between numerous homes, creating bedlam and a void during mealtime.

Managing a chaotic calendar, communication with the former spouse, hectic school schedules, shopping, and all of the normal Christmas frenzy can turn the season created to draw us closer to God into a nightmare.

Tip #78 The Best Predictor of the Future—The Past

Preparing before the holidays arrive is a key element to stopping the madness. It's wise to sit down with your spouse and map out a plan on how to keep the priorities straight.

At this moment I hear stepmoms all over the world screaming, "That would be a great idea if we didn't have to work our life around his ex-wife and her last-minute decisions. We can't make plans because she refuses to communicate with us. When we do set up a schedule she changes everything at the last minute. It's so frustrating."

If past experience has revealed that the former spouse has a tendency to uproot and change the holiday plans at the last minute, assume that she will do it again this year. Lower your expectations, learn from the past, and prepare a plan B for her attempt to ruin your holiday. Learn the things you can control, and let go of the things you cannot. If your husband decides he cannot handle her behavior any longer, the first step is for him to speak calmly with her and suggest a compromise that is beneficial for everyone, including the children. If she refuses, then his only recourse is to go back to court.

However, as the stepmom the only way to minimize your stress is to create a schedule with the assumption that you may face upheaval.

Tip #79 Create New Memories

A common trap that many stepmoms fall into is attempting to resurrect a ghost from Christmas past. I'm not suggesting it's wise to toss out former traditions; what I am recommending is a family brainstorming session.

I suggest your husband open the conversation with questions such as: "How would you like to do something new this year for Christmas? What are some of the traditions that are important to you that you'd like to maintain? What are some suggestions on how we can have more fun this year?"

Allow the kids to offer input regarding the things they like, dislike, and may not have considered yet. The goal is to create fresh memories and yet maintain the traditions that are significant for each family member.

Tip #80 Address Favoritism

"My mother buys my two girls lavish gifts at Christmas and on birthdays. I now have two stepdaughters around the same ages. The gifts she buys my husband's children are trinkets and considerably less expensive. Although I don't want the kids to think Christmas is all about dollar signs, my stepdaughters are hurt when they open the presents. I've tried explaining this to my mom but she doesn't see the problem. It's creating tension within our home."

In this scenario the mom is refusing to accept how her favoritism is harming her daughter's home. Therefore, the stepmom will need to make it clearer and implement a boundary with her mother such as limiting time together. It's very possible that Grandma doesn't understand the sibling rivalry that can erupt when blending two families.

However, it's also important to remember that in-laws have a deeper connection to their own biological family. They should not be expected to immediately embrace or bond with children they barely know. There is a fine line between shunning or favoritism and a lack of connection. It's important to communicate and allow all family members to voice an opinion.

Weddings

Tip #81 Lower Your Expectations

"My stepdaughter and I have had a fantastic relationship since I married her dad seven years ago. She just got engaged and all of a sudden she is treating me as though I have leprosy. I'm so excited about her upcoming marriage, and I even offered to throw her a bridal shower. But that has caused her to back away from me even more. I don't understand. What happened?"

This is a question I have received from numerous stepmoms who have an adult stepdaughter. Many times the stepmom has played a significant role in the life of this young woman, and the relationship between the two has gone very well. However, once an engagement ring slides onto the stepdaughter's finger she may step back—way back—from a stepmom.

The most common reason for this is a fear of offending or upsetting the biological mom. Picking out a wedding gown and veil and planning the glorious event creates a bond between mother and daughter. It's often a moment they have dreamed about since the stepdaughter was a child. Even if the relationship with the biological mother is strained, it's not uncommon for a daughter to view this magical moment of bridal hoopla as a way for her to reunite and reconnect with her mother.

Tip #82 Step Aside: A Gift to Your Husband and His Kids

When my stepsons got married I decided the greatest gift I could give them was to stay on the sidelines. I learned this from my own first wedding while dealing with extensive tension between my mother, father, and stepmother. Decisions regarding who would sit where without getting offended and who would pay for what, along with the dilemma over family photos, made the day stressful and difficult for me. I chose not to do that to my stepsons.

When they got engaged I told my oldest stepson and his fiancée, "I want this to be a wonderful day for you. I don't want you to be worried about stepfamily issues. If you want your dad and mom in pictures together with you, I am happy to step out of those pictures without any offense. Every child should have the gift of having their mom and dad surrounding them on their wedding day. If you would like me to do something for you, or if you want me to be a part of the wedding, I'm happy to do it. But I don't need to be included. This is your day; I want it to be about you." And I meant it.

At my oldest stepson's wedding, he and his wife asked me to sing "The Lord's Prayer"; at the nuptials for my younger stepson, he and his wife asked me to read a Bible verse. I was delighted to comply in each situation. But I did not force myself into that setting because I understand the mind of an adult child of divorce on their wedding day. For that one day they long for their parents to behave maturely. They wish to have one blissful memory where Mom and Dad, the two people who brought them into the world, stand side by side without fighting. They crave unity as they celebrate the greatest day of their lives.

Stepmom, will you give your stepchild this precious gift? The day is not about you or the role you played in the life of this child. The real question is will you love this child enough to give them a day without tension, stress, choosing sides, or thinking about how to please everyone else? I guarantee it is the greatest present you can give. Even if your stepchild doesn't recognize or appreciate the sacrifice—your husband will. It will be tucked away in his mind as one of the reasons he loves his wife.

Tip #83 Find an Ally

If the wedding is going to be unusually stressful, and the stepmom already feels like an outsider, an important step is for her to find at least one person to stand by her side. This might be a family member, a friend, or the pastor's wife. If the stepmom has at least one person that she feels is a confidante, she will be much more relaxed.

Sometimes that person comes from the in-law side of the wedding. My stepdaughter-in-law Julie introduces me as her mother-in-law. And I introduce her as my daughter-in-law. I never say stepdaughter-in-law because I've been a part of her life since she met, dated, got engaged, and married my stepson. She and I have never known any other relationship. Sometimes I feel closer to her than I do my stepson—her husband.

Mother's Day

"As soon as the advertisements for Mother's Day flowers start appearing, I get discouraged," stepmom Jackie sighed. "It's one of the worst days of the year for me."

If there's a holiday that can cause a stepmom to weep, it's Mother's Day. That's because a stepmom has all of the work, responsibilities, financial strain, carpooling, laundry, dishes, and tears of a biological mom, but she rarely has the recognition and appreciation.

Tip #84 Explain Your Expectations

I used to get very upset about Mother's Day. I never expected my stepsons to honor me because they have a mother, and it is not me. However, I anticipated that my husband would do something special in appreciation for the blood, sweat, and tears I have experienced while trying to be a good stepmom to his children. The problem was he didn't know it. I would get mad and hurt when he didn't offer to do something special for me on the holiday.

Finally, I realized that I needed to help him "connect the dots." Once I explained to Steve that I expected him to do something nice for me, he was more than willing. I learned a good lesson. Sometimes my husband doesn't see things through the same lens that I do. And it's foolish for me to become angry with him or to shut down emotionally when a simple conversation can eradicate the problem.

If after you share these feelings with your spouse, he is still unwilling to honor you on Mother's Day, that is a marital concern and an issue of respect more than it is a stepfamily problem.

Educating the Church

"I avoid church on Mother's Day," stepmom Karen explained. "I just hate the awkward moment when the pastor asks the mothers to stand up. I never know what to do. My husband views me as a mom to his kids, but I know his children don't see me that way. So it's just easier not to attend that morning."

Isn't that sad?

Over the years my friend and coauthor Ron Deal and I have attempted to help the church understand the unique circumstances surrounding stepfamilies. "Just use the word stepmom," Ron tells pastors, "and you validate her as an important caregiver in her home."[1]

Sometimes it's necessary for a stepmom to inform others how she feels about Mother's Day. For each woman it will be different. The common denominator is that most stepmoms have some type of issue to deal with on Mother's Day.

Vacations

Traveling as a stepfamily can create various obstacles. The level of "Brady Bunch" expectations is heightened, and the attempt to meet everyone's needs can become grueling.

Tip #85 Work Toward New Traditions

A stepmom usually exhausts herself trying to prepare, pack, and keep everyone happy during a vacation. In addition, you may feel an overwhelming burden to create special memories now that you have formed a new family. It's important to remember that starting new traditions and pleasant experiences together as a stepfamily doesn't happen instantly. You don't need to cram every dream into one summer vacation. But you can take baby steps toward creating times together that will stir fond memories in the future.

The key is to let the fun times happen naturally. Many of the times that my stepfamily fondly reminisces and laughs about now were the spontaneous things we did together.

Steve's sons and I still crack up over the time when their dad went into a store to buy a newspaper and I moved the car. We were in hysterics while watching his perplexed expressions when he couldn't find the car. He didn't think it was funny, and we didn't let him suffer for long, but it's an example of a great memory his sons and I enjoy together.

Tip #86 Create Privacy and Personal Space

"I loathe stepfamily vacations, and my stepmom friends do as well," Cynthia shared. "It feels as though I never get a moment alone to breathe. And although my husband and I would love to have a few romantic moments together, being surrounded by both sets of children makes that impossible."

When my husband and I take a stepfamily vacation, I purposely plan a few short "time-outs" for myself. If I don't spend a little time away from the crowd to fill my own tank, I become miserable. After the first vacation disaster, I learned to explain this to my husband beforehand so he would not think I was angry or retreating.

Now that we are dealing with older children, if at all possible he and I carve out brief sections of the vacation where it is just the two of us. If you have younger kids that cannot be left alone, it might be worth looking into traveling with another family or bringing a teenager along who can baby-sit so that you get a breather.

Tip #87 Learn Why the Kids Don't Care

"My husband and I planned a wonderful vacation to visit my parents, who live on a lake," stepmom Christina explained. "It included his kids (who love water sports), my children, and my extended family. I knew this was going to be the best vacation ever as we all enjoy the water, plus my family's home is wonderfully cozy. After months of planning and a great deal of expense, my husband's kids backed out at the last minute. I was furious and embarrassed. I didn't know what to tell my family."

It's not uncommon for a family vacation to be more important for the stepmom than it is the stepkids. They often don't feel a need to bond with the stepsiblings or the stepmom's family. Sometimes those things occur naturally if the stepmom's family lives nearby and they have continuous contact with them. However, planning a vacation with the stepmom's family as the nucleus can backfire. That is because the stepchildren already have enough extended family, and they do not see the need to make the stepmom's family a priority. It is not necessarily a reflection on the stepmom and likely has nothing to do with her. It is merely that they are not invested in developing these relationships or creating stepfamily memories.

A few years ago my stepfamily returned to our hometown for a family vacation. We all live in different parts of the United States, and we decided it might be fun to go back and reminisce with those who still live in our former community. This included visiting my brother and his large extended family.

Although my stepsons know my brother and his adult kids a little, due to logistics they hadn't seen them in many years. I wondered if my stepsons, their wives, and their kids would feel uncomfortable. Shortly after we arrived, it became obvious that everyone was getting along great. My brother and my oldest stepson both like mechanical things, so they chatted about manly stuff such as tools and cars. My youngest stepson inserted several of his witty jokes. One was a risky reference to yellow crime scene tape and an unusual relative, which had us laughing so hard it hurt. The women gathered around and strung beads to make necklaces and conversed about girly things. Even my granddaughter made a new friend with my niece's stepdaughter, who is the same age.

It was a magnificent moment.

I mentally stepped back and looked around the room at this group of people who really don't know each other, and yet are connected through my marriage to Steve. The realization hit that to some degree we finally had bonded as a family. They don't send Christmas cards to each other or call on birthdays. But that day we sat around my brother's house, laughed, and reminisced as one family.

In my opinion this is a successful stepfamily.

My situation didn't happen overnight, and each stepfamily experience is unique. But in the end, it's been worth it. The key is to remain on a steady course of working toward unification.

☙〇❧

Holy God, I believe that over time you can heal the wounds and the scars that were created by divorce, grief, or loss in our family. You can bestow a blessing over the place where death or divorce attempted to steal our joy.

Thank you for your faithfulness. Create in me a clean heart so that I may be an ambassador of your grace, mercy, and compassion in every circumstance.

Fill my chaotic mind with your peace, transform my negative attitudes into gratitude, and convert my weaknesses into your strength. I need you to be my source of wisdom. Provide me with your perfect timing and tenderness. Let my face, my eyes, and my touch be a reflection of your image.

Suggested Bible verses:
Joel 2:25; Ecclesiastes 7:8; Psalm 51:10–11; Jeremiah 29:7

9

Let's Hear It From the Men— Hubby's Perspective

It is easier to build strong children than to repair broken men.

—Frederick Douglass

Fathers, do not exasperate your children; instead, bring them up in the training and instruction of the Lord.

—Paul, tentmaker,
apostle to the non-Jews (Gentiles)

I can't win," a dad stated. "If my wife is happy, my children feel as though I'm siding with her. And if I do what my children want, then my wife feels as though I'm not standing beside her. No matter what I do it's wrong, and somebody gets hurt. I'm in a no-win situation."

This is the way many dads who remarry view stepfamily living. They wish everyone understood how trapped they feel in the tug-of-war. When I coach stepfamilies, the dad often shares his angst, frustration, and despair over the fact that he is constantly torn between his wife and his children.

Although it sounds obvious, numerous husbands long for their wives to believe "I married you because I love you, and I know you are a good stepmother to my children. I don't regret marrying you; you are the love of my life. I really want to make this marriage work. I also love my children, and I don't want to lose them." These emotions are at the root of the husband's actions. In other words, he merely wants his wife to understand how trapped in the middle he genuinely feels. Husbands often share that stepfamily life took them by complete surprise, and blending two families has been much more work than they anticipated. At my stepmom retreats, we offer an entire workshop that helps a stepmom see the stepfamily through her husband's eyes (www.SisterhoodofStepmoms.com).

Here is what many husbands wish they could say to their wives.

Tip #88 "I Have No Desire to Reconcile With My Ex-Wife"

There is a secret fear that numerous stepmoms share. They wonder if deep inside their husband's heart he wishes he were still married to his former wife. Truth be told, this is rarely true.

It's not uncommon for a stepmom to ponder, "Was his first wife a better cook, lover, or partner?" If those thoughts become all-consuming, it can lead to tension in the marriage. The husband feels as though he must constantly affirm his loyalty and love. This becomes tedious and causes him to think his wife is never going to believe that she's his priority.

It's important for a stepmom to discern whether she is having these feelings because of her own insecurities or her husband's behavior. If hubby is keeping secrets, hiding money, or spending an excessive amount of time with his former spouse, there may be reason for concern. Sometimes determining what is behind his actions requires obtaining the opinion of an impartial third party. It's possible that neither spouse recognizes how their actions are causing a problem.

Tip #89 "I Know This Is Harder Than We Thought It Would Be"

"I feel as though I have ruined my wife's life by bringing her into this stepfamily," Charles, a dad of three, stated. "Before our marriage she laughed a lot and was so carefree. Now she is stressed all the time, and I find her crying."

When a couple remarries they are often ambushed by the difficult issues that arise. This can cause the husband to wonder if his wife is regretting the decision to marry him. And to be honest, sometimes she does feel that way. This is normal.

A marriage will not thrive under this heavy weight of guilt. It's important for the couple to openly communicate while including an affirmation that they are committed to the marriage. This builds trust and well-being within the union and eliminates the fear that one partner might desert the marriage.

Tip #90 "I'm Scared"

After a divorce it's not uncommon for a dad to parent out of guilt, fear, or shame. In addition, he may be worried that he will lose his children to the former wife and possibly a new stepdad. All of these negative emotions can prevent him from setting the necessary boundaries with his children. The kids quickly learn how to wrap Dad around their finger, and he caters to their every whim. This creates self-centered children who are unpleasant to be around.

If a stepmom isn't careful she can become critical and emasculating as opposed to helpful. It's important for her to weigh her words and the tone of her voice carefully. This was a mistake I made early in my marriage. I thought I was being helpful to point out the areas where my husband's kids needed instruction. But he interpreted my comments as belittling and nitpicking. My words didn't encourage him to be a better father; instead they made him feel like a failure as a parent, and this created tension in our marriage.

Stepfamily expert Ron Deal helped me to understand some of the reasons why dads respond the way they do. He shares, "One reason dads may disengage is because they are puzzled by child rearing and development and just aren't sure what to do. They love their children immensely but aren't equipped with discipline strategies and practical tools for parenting."[1] In other words, they are scared.

This is particularly true if they had a father who parented poorly:

> Fathers with little education about child development, discipline, punishment, and the spiritual development of children often feel puzzled about how to parent. They don't engage because they don't know how. . . . It is unfamiliar territory; they don't know how to navigate the terrain, so they pull back or stumble through. . . . Typically we learn how to parent from our parents.[2]

If your husband is confused, intimidated, or terrified of parenting, it's advisable for the two of you to read books or watch DVDs on parenting, and attend parenting classes that will put his emotions to rest. In those classes he will meet other fathers who feel the same way. This should calm his anxiety over the role of fatherhood and allow both of you to meet other couples who face similar challenges.

Tip #91 "I'm Afraid of Losing My Kids"

"I know my ex-wife walks all over me, but I have no choice," David, a newly married dad, stated. "If I don't let her make all the rules she threatens to withhold my kids from me. She has done it in the past so I know it can happen. Since I remarried it's gotten worse. My former wife hates my new wife with a passion, and she tries to make our lives as miserable as possible. I know it drives my wife crazy that I won't stand up to my ex, but I can't risk losing my kids."

My heart aches for any man in this situation. He wants to be a good dad, and he desires to implement a boundary with his former spouse. However, when he does the situation becomes a war. The key here is to evaluate what is a necessary boundary to keep the marriage intact and yet still maintain a working relationship with the ex. When the ex-wife is unwilling to co-parent in a healthy way, this becomes extremely difficult.

If your husband sets up a time to sit down privately with his former spouse and calmly reviews the common goal of raising healthy, emotionally stable children, sometimes they can come to a truce. If not, you and he will need to determine how to continue having a healthy, active relationship with his children and yet not allow the other home to destroy the current marriage. The book *Co-Parenting Works* by Tammy Daughtry can provide additional insight on how to work toward healthy strategies. It is written from the perspective of a single mom, not a stepfamily; however, it provides good insight on co-parenting strategies.

Tip #92 "I Just Want Peace"

I began to disrespect my husband, Steve, when he wouldn't stand up to his ex-wife. It felt like he was more concerned with keeping everyone else happy than he was standing his ground.

To me he appeared cowardly and pathetic. In reality he was merely attempting to keep peace.

Husband Andy Hetchler explains:

> Your partner is aware that his acts can be a source of stress for you and, if he's being nice to his former spouse or not rocking the boat, most likely he is doing that to keep the peace and minimize a storm from blowing in from her house into yours. While it may appear at times that your man is giving in to his ex, he is really giving you peace and putting his love and desire for you above his need to stand his ground with her. When weighing the costs versus the benefits, men typically will take a minor loss of finances, schedule, etc., to gain peace in the home.[3]

In other words, when a wife assumes her husband to be spineless, he may be just the opposite. It's possible that he is trying to protect his wife from more unnecessary drama. He is willing to ignore things that he views as minor in order to keep the peace. There is a fine line between being a peacemaker and a peaceaholic. I'm not saying that your husband should tiptoe around his former spouse. For each family this will play out differently.

Tip #93 "I Don't Think or Parent Like You Do"

It's almost impossible for couples to agree on every single parenting issue. This is particularly true in a stepfamily. Most husbands desire to hear the stepmom's perspective on how to parent, and what they may be doing wrong. How a wife approaches her husband regarding the things she perceives he needs to change makes all the difference in his willingness and his attitude. When a man feels he has disappointed his wife it's hard on him, and he doesn't like being told that he is doing a bad job. In other words, he can't hear what you're saying because of the way you're saying it.

It's a good idea to wait until the emotions over an issue have calmed down and a couple can communicate without becoming angry or frustrated. Picking when and where to discuss the problem is crucial. For example, the minute a husband walks through the door after a stressful day at work or right after a confrontation with his ex-wife is not the time to start a heated conversation. Chances are it will not go well, and there is a strong possibility a husband will emotionally shut down and not hear anything his wife has to say. It's not that he isn't interested, but merely a factor related to feelings of failure or the sense of being overwhelmed that causes him to retreat.

It should go without saying that these conversations should never take place in front of the children. If the kids see their dad and his wife arguing over how to parent, it may cause them to fear that this marriage may also end in divorce. The opposite might also occur. Hearing the fight might prompt the perspective that they are winning the battle to "divide and conquer" their dad's relationship with his wife.

When tackling these difficult situations it's important to accept that men and women see things differently. It took me a long time to realize that I needed to stop trying to make Steve like me. He sees things through a man's lens, which is radically different than a woman's. His methods of communication are unlike mine.

I became convicted that instead of loving my husband for the way he was created, I was trying to mold him into something else. This was a huge mistake. Steve is never going to be like me. And that's a good thing. God packed his luggage in an entirely different format than he did mine. When I began to embrace and appreciate the good things about my husband, such as his strong character, his honesty and integrity, and his unconditional love for me, our dissimilarities began to diminish.

Sometimes I still get frustrated with his lack of communication skills, or his inability to find the half gallon of milk sitting in plain sight on the refrigerator shelf. There are times that I wish he would speak up and say certain things to his sons that I view as beneficial. But I've learned that I'm not his mother and it's not my job to correct him. Occasionally, I will make a suggestion or ask a question that might prompt him to think differently. True love requires that I accept our differences. This has gone a long way toward making our home harmonious.

Tip #94 "Sometimes You Make the Situation Worse"

It's time for stepmoms to admit that sometimes we throw gasoline on the flame of stepfamily drama. There are times when the temptation to have the last word or throw a jab at the ex-wife feels too good to ignore.

You will know you're becoming a smart stepmom when nasty words appear in your mind, but before you speak them you hit the pause button on your tongue. In that moment you consider how the whole thing is going to end. You review the disappointed expression on your husband's face, the look of rejection in your stepchild's eyes, or a flashback memory of the last time you said something malicious to the former spouse. And the images stop you from spewing snippy comments. Stepmom, bring out the pom-poms and cheer because you are on the road to stepfamily victory. Take my word for it, the peace and the satisfaction that come from taking the high road, and keeping your mouth shut, are worth it.

Your husband will respect you for making the life of his child easier. And isn't earning his respect better than inflicting a momentary blow on his former spouse?

Tip #95 "Please Be Patient With My Kids"

For a stepmom, working toward a relationship with the children often takes time and a great deal of patience. I know in my own circumstance I had more patience with my own nieces than I did my stepsons. This is a common denominator among many stepmoms. The ability to allow for failure is readily available to those in our own family. However, a stepmom's frustration fuse can be short with her stepchildren. Perhaps it is because she is a bit more tense when the stepkids come for visitation or she has pent-up anger and frustration over other related issues. Regardless of the reasons, her husband truly wants her to be more patient with his children.

If you find yourself becoming short-tempered or overly demanding with his kids, it's a good idea to take a stepfamily time-out. I learned to step away from tense situations by going to another room or outside and taking a deep breath. Then I asked myself a few questions, such as, "Why is this bothering me so much?" or I began to pray, "Lord, help me to see these children through your eyes. Help me to recognize if I'm being too harsh. Help me to be gentler with them. Teach me to remember that they are just kids. I don't want to do anything that would crush their spirits or damage their self-esteem. I need discernment and wisdom on how to handle the situation." Normally after a few minutes alone I could evaluate the conflict from a clearer perspective and know whether or not to apologize. I asked myself, "In a year from now, will this problem matter? Is it important enough to stand my ground?"

If the issue is related to the child's character building, respect, honesty, or morality, it may be worth standing firm. But things such as setting the table, making the bed perfectly, or filling the dishwasher properly might not be worth the argument. This is where it is different for a stepmom and a biological mom. Sometimes it's hard to discern whether the anger is misplaced due to stepfamily frustrations or the issue is truly something that needs to be addressed with the child. Often a third party who understands stepfamily complexities, and is not emotionally attached to the situation, is necessary. Many of my life coaching clients come to me for help to discover the best way to handle an ongoing frustration.

Remember that for a stepmom, building the relationship with her stepkids is the key goal. This does not mean ignoring or tolerating rude or disrespectful behavior. Civil and respectful conduct should be required from everyone in the home. It does mean that perhaps she might have to overlook less important issues. There is no Band-Aid or cookie-cutter answer to the numerous tensions and difficult situations that arise for the stepmom.

In conclusion, focusing on unity, commitment, healthy boundaries, and wise conflict resolution is vitally important to keep the marriage alive.

Marital issues such as alcoholism, physical or emotional abuse, manipulation and control tactics, pornography, threats, drug addiction, or other destructive patterns require more extensive assistance. I highly recommend the book *The Emotionally Destructive Marriage* by Leslie Vernick. Plus it is advisable to visit a therapist and/or support group that understand the complex and caustic behaviors associated with these patterns. When left unaddressed, these hurtful actions combined with normal stepfamily complexities spell a formula for disaster. Ignoring the issues will not make them disappear; it merely prolongs the pain for the couple and the children.

∞o∞

Almighty Father, I need you. It is the desire of my heart that I be a support and encouragement to my husband. Give me the ears to hear, and a clear mind to accept, the male perspective on living in a stepfamily.

Provide insight on the areas where I am making the situation worse. And I lift my hands in gratitude to you for the times when I choose higher ground. I thank you for giving me the strength and the wisdom to do the right thing even when it would momentarily feel so good to throw a hissy fit.

Thank you for being the Great Teacher. I desire to be teachable. Protect my marriage from the forces of evil that threaten to destroy us. Put your shield of fortification over us as a family. You are the victorious warrior. I rest in the shelter of your mighty wing.

You long for my marriage and my family to be strong and healthy even more than I do. Your Word tells me that you will not withhold anything good if I choose to honor you and keep you in the center of my life and home.

Suggested Bible verses:
John 10:10; Matthew 7:28–29; Psalm 84:10–12; 91

10

Mirror, Mirror on the Wall—
A Peek Inside

I don't know the key to success, but the key to failure
is trying to please everybody.

—Bill Cosby

He has sent me to bind up the brokenhearted, to pro-
claim freedom for the captives and release from darkness for the prisoners, . . . to bestow on them a crown
of beauty instead of ashes . . . and a garment of praise
instead of a spirit of despair.

—Isaiah, the greatest Old Testament prophet,
spoke specific details of the coming Messiah
700 years before Christ was born

S everal years into my second marriage I discovered that
some of my marital problems had nothing to do with Steve
or his kids. The issues were really about—me. I had colossal

emotional baggage in my own life that I never knew existed until God gently and patiently pulled back a curtain of lies and revealed the truth.

Up to that point I had no idea why I was plagued with anxiety and fear, and a foreboding sense that doom was around the corner. As I began to heal from childhood issues, I discovered a twisted codependent way of thinking that dwelled within me. Before this revelation I had a distorted view of the word *codependency*. I pictured a weak, timid woman, cowering in the corner, who is married to an alcoholic or abuser. Since I am an outgoing person with a strong personality, I falsely assumed that I couldn't be an enabler.

I was wrong.

My affliction can be described in a variety of ways, including enabler, people pleaser, fixer, rescuer, or codependent. The words may be different, but the meaning is basically the same. People with timid personalities can be people pleasers, but so can those with gregarious traits similar to mine. The toxic conundrum is related to childhood more than personality type. I took a good long look in the mirror and realized that I could be the poster child for Codependency Anonymous.

What does enabling have to do with stepmoms? Take a peek at the most common inquiries I receive from stepmoms. See if you can determine what each one has in common.

"How can I get . . ."

- my husband to stand up to his kids
- the biological mom to stop saying horrible things about me
- my stepkids to respect me
- my in-laws to accept me
- my husband to spend time alone with me
- his kids to go to church
- the stepkids to appreciate all that I do for them

- my husband to see my pain and loneliness
- the biological mom to inform me on issues

Perhaps you hear yourself asking similar questions. Maybe reading them from the perspective of another stepmom helps you see the problem.

When a sentence begins with the phrase "How can I get," there is a good chance it's coming from someone who struggles with codependency or enabling. It's an indication they are attempting to control a circumstance they cannot. The reality is that I can't force a person to do anything. I do not have that much power over another human being. Here's the additional news flash that should bring relief—it's not my job! It's God's job to change people. Typically, my role is to get out of the way and set appropriate boundaries with the individual.

My job is to allow the offender to experience discomfort when they make a poor choice. The truth is, our human nature often refuses to see the light until our faces are deep into the darkness and yuck of the mud caused by foolish decisions. The Bible clarifies it this way: "Before I went through suffering, I went down the wrong path. But now I obey your word. You are good, and what you do is good. Teach me your orders. . . . It was good for me to suffer. That's what helped me to understand your orders" (Psalm 119:67–68, 71).

Do you hear the psalmist say, "It was good" for him to suffer affliction? That's because it's the pain that brought him to his senses and repentance. This triggered him to turn the destructive choices into prudent ones. In other words, after suffering the consequences of his poor choices he shifted from foolishness to wisdom.

It's important to stress that the healthy, unselfish, and godly goal for implementing a consequence should always be the desire for a loved one to repent and turn around. An unloving boundary is when manipulation, control, or shame is used to punish the person.

Impure hearts use boundaries to act out feelings such as revenge and anger. Because none of us is pure, we have to search our motives for establishing boundaries to make sure that they serve love and not our impure motives. Using distance or withdrawal of love, for example, to punish the other is a sign that we are setting boundaries not to resolve the conflict, but to get revenge.[1]

Under the best of circumstances, setting limitations can be uncomfortable. Stepfamilies may struggle even more due to the guilt, shame, and complexities surrounding the stepfamily life. Dad and stepmom often don't know how to set reasonable boundaries when co-parenting between two homes.

Many of the complex issues associated with stepfamilies involve poor choices made by a spouse, biological parent, or stepkids. All of these situations are out of the stepmom's control. Therefore, it is absolutely crucial for her to understand the root causes of controlling and enabling behaviors. Life as a stepmom will likely propel any tendencies toward codependency into full-throttle overdrive.

Tip #96 Explore Whether You Are an Enabler

In my book *When "I Do" Becomes "I Don't": Practical Steps for Healing During Separation and Divorce,* I share Pat Springle's definition of codependency:

> A compulsion to control and rescue people by fixing their problems. It occurs when a person's God-given needs for love and security have been blocked in a relationship with a dysfunctional person, resulting in a lack of objectivity, a warped sense of responsibility, being controlled and controlling others.[2]

Have you ever been confronted with the possibility of being a people pleaser? Maybe this chapter has revealed a new perspective on the subject of enabling. Perhaps you're a bit confused.

Doesn't the Bible say that we're supposed to be peacemakers? *New York Times* bestselling author Rick Warren clarifies,

> Jesus didn't say, "Blessed are the peace lovers," because everyone *loves* peace. Neither did he say, "Blessed are the peaceable," who are never disturbed by anything. Jesus said, "Blessed are those who *work* for peace"—those who actively seek to resolve conflict. Peacemakers are rare because peacemaking is hard work.[3]

Tip #97 Confess Your Weakness

If you've ever watched Dr. Phil McGraw on TV, it's likely you've heard him say, "You can't change what you don't acknowledge."[4] And I agree. The first step in healing my need to please was admitting that I have a problem. It's vitally important to step out of denial and stop saying, "I'm just too nice." That's a subtle and manipulative way of labeling codependency as a virtue. Enabling is not being nice; it's a destructive pattern that intensifies with each passing generation.

Being a peacemaker does not mean avoiding conflict. Pretending a problem doesn't exist doesn't identify a hero, it reveals a coward.

Rick Warren continues to explain, "Jesus, the Prince of Peace, was never afraid of conflict. On occasion he *provoked* it for the good of everyone."[5]

Tip #98 Find the Root Reasons

When I was five years old my brother was born. He was very ill and almost died. That traumatic event, followed by my parents' divorce three years later, is how my tendency toward codependency and enabling began. I was thrust into an adult role at a very young age. After my parents separated I have six months of memory loss. Before the separation I can envision numerous things such as my bedroom wallpaper, the plaid on our couch, and where the Tide box was stored in our bathroom. But I cannot recall leaving our little apartment, changing schools, or moving in with my aunt and uncle. My little eight-year-old brain shut down because it was incapable of handling the trauma.

In my thirties, during a season of counseling, I learned that I blamed myself for my parents' divorce. This is most likely the reason for my memory loss. It's also the reason I carried a great deal of shame, fear, loneliness, and guilt into my teens and early adulthood. I came by codependency very innocently. Most people do.

A person can become codependent for any number of reasons. Almost all of these patterns can be traced to a problem in the home while growing up. The following list, while not complete, explains some of the most common causes.

- Alcoholism or drugs anywhere within the family. (This includes grandparents, stepparents, siblings, cousins, etc.)
- Physical abuse: beatings, spitting, biting, slapping in the face, being locked in the closet, etc.
- Emotional abuse, including insults, intense criticism, being told "You were never wanted," or "You are stupid," etc.
- Sexual abuse by a relative, neighbor, or a close friend of the family
- Parents with extensive mental disorders
- Parents who were physically ill and unavailable
- Parents who were emotionally unavailable
- Parents who were absent due to a divorce or workaholism
- Parents who were unpredictable and yelled, screamed, and accused with no explanation
- Parents who used the child as a substitute for a mate
- Parents who coddled or overprotected the child
- Parents who expected perfection or had unrealistic standards[6]

It makes sense that when our needs were not met as children, we gravitated toward someone or something to fill that void. "The more deeply one has been wounded, the higher the probability that one will be codependent. The pain from the past leaks into the present," states John P. Splinter.[7]

When I finally woke up and got help for my enabling issues, I became a better wife, stepmom, daughter, sister, friend, etc. I'm not completely cured. There are still times and issues that can activate and launch my people-pleasing cycle. Extended time with my family can be a common trigger because it feels normal to revert back into old familiar patterns.

What I thought were acts of compassion and love were in reality the opposite. Isn't it merciful to shield a loved one from suffering discomfort? Often the answer is no. Sometimes the most loving thing I can do for another person is to allow them to suffer a consequence when they make a sinful or poor choice.

Discovering the root causes has helped me to unveil the hidden lies that held me captive for so long. Unveiling those lies took away their power and set me on a journey to freedom. It can do the same for you.

Tip #99 Learn How Codependency Has Affected Your Life

If you recognize a battle with codependency and enabling, it's time to explore how it has manifested into your life and decisions. For me, rescuing everyone had become my identity. I felt it was the only thing that made me special or valuable. And if God healed me from rescuing other people from their problems, and I let them suffer a consequence, then what would my purpose be? This stirred a tremendous amount of fear. Letting go of the familiar, even if it's unhealthy or destructive, can be terrifying.

Enabling looks and feels as though it's helping another, but in reality it's selfish. I'm a people pleaser because it meets a need in me, or I wouldn't keep doing it. Enabling is frequently rooted in fear and the need to control our surroundings and other people.

When I finally surrendered and admitted that I had an issue—dare I say an addiction—of rescuing others, my identity came under attack. The strangulating tentacles of enabling weren't going down without a fight. It was war.

Tip #100 Take Steps to Heal

What are you willing to do to stop the cycle? Here are a few suggestions:

- Attend a Celebrate Recovery support group. To find a group near you, go to www.celebraterecovery.com.
- Obtain resources such as *The Emotionally Destructive Relationship* by Leslie Vernick, *No More Christian Nice Girl* by Paul Coughlin and Jennifer Degler, and *Waking the Dead* by John Eldredge.
- Find a therapist who specializes in codependency issues.

Tip #101 Discover the Difference Between Healthy Boundaries and Improper Consequences

It is possible to begin setting boundaries with wrong motives and improper methods. When thoughts such as, "I'll get back at you," "I'm going to make you suffer," or "I'm going to show you how ugly things can get around here" begin to surface, that's an indication that the attempt to stop the madness is being fueled by unhealthy thinking. Before implementing a consequence, take a moment to consider some indications that you might be setting boundaries for the wrong reasons or in an inappropriate manner. Asking a trusted friend, a marriage mentor, or a therapist who understands enabling behaviors for feedback may be a good option.

Obviously in this complex world there are additional issues other than codependency that can create a wounded soul. However, I have discovered that codependency is one of the root reasons that marriages end in divorce. That is why I have devoted an entire chapter to the topic. If you would like to read more information on how enabling can affect your life and marriage, I suggest *Boundaries in Marriage* by Henry Cloud and John Townsend or *Bold Love* by Dan Allender.

∽⟋0⟍∽

Lord, I understand that I cannot control my spouse, his former wife, or my stepchildren. I confess that fear may be causing me to dominate situations and the loved ones in my life that in actuality belong only to you.

Teach me how to overcome my obsession to fix everything. Reveal how the need to please became rooted in my life so that I can begin healing. I am unable to do this on my own. Please show me how. If this requires professional therapy, teach me how to be willing to take that step. And crush any pride that might stop me from obtaining freedom. I desperately long to be free from the affliction of codependency and the burden it has placed on my life. I am not responsible for how the problem formed, but I am now responsible to step out of the destructive cycle and find healing in you. Amen.

Suggested Bible verses:
Psalm 34:4–6; 120:6–7; Romans 12:1–2

11

Who's Your Daddy? Satisfying Our Deepest Longing

Hope knows that if great trials are avoided great deeds
remain undone and the possibility of growth into great-
ness of soul is aborted.

—Brennan Manning

I have loved you with an everlasting love.

—Jeremiah, the weeping prophet

Imagine a person who has never tasted a lemon asking, "What
does a lemon taste like?" How would you describe it? Does
anything else taste like a lemon? No. You have to taste it—to
experience it. An intimacy with the Creator of the universe is
very similar. You have to experience it, really taste it, to know
what it's like.

My spiritual expedition has been like Mr. Toad's wild ride
at Disney. I'm somewhat of a church mutt. Let me explain. I

was raised in the Catholic church, where I gratefully learned a reverence for God. In my early twenties I visited a small Pentecostal church with my brother, where I encountered a God who desires a relationship with me. It was there that I accepted and believed that Jesus Christ is who he claims to be—the Savior of the world. During that season I learned to trust his declaration, "I am the way and the truth and the life. No one comes to the Father [in other words gets into heaven] except through me."[1] And for seventeen years I attended a Baptist church, where I explored the Bible and learned how its teachings are relevant and practical for my day-to-day life.

A move to Orlando placed my husband and me in a very large nondenominational congregation. In that setting I observed how to reach out to the community for Christ. A move to Georgia placed us in a Wesleyan church. Later a pastor friend was planting a new Presbyterian (PCA) church and asked us to join him, so we attended this denomination for a while to determine if that was God's leading. After a job loss we moved back to Florida, where my husband went on staff at a Methodist church. Wow! What an expedition.

I call myself a Catho-bapticostal-nondenominational-presbywesleyist. This kaleidoscope of church experiences taught me a significant spiritual lesson. God doesn't reside in a denomination, but rather in the hearts of his people. I believe this divine journey was God's training camp in preparation for my present ministry of writing and speaking. Whether people are worshiping in a traditional high mass, jumping over the pews, or somewhere in between, I sense God's presence.

A new perspective resulted from all the bouncing. I found a common denominator lurking in the pews. Underneath all the singing, Bible reading, hand clapping, and potluck suppers, I discovered that many people who attend church do not believe God loves them. If asked, "Do you believe God loves you?" they would answer with an affirming yes! But tweak the question to

"What do you think God sees when he looks at you?" or worse yet, "Do you think God likes you?" and the squirming begins.

Behind closed doors the lie prowling deep inside the heart is exposed. We may profess John 3:16: "God loved the world so much that he gave his one and only Son. Anyone who believes in him will not die but have eternal life." However, in the caverns of our soul lurks the reality that we don't truly believe God's unconditional love is meant for—me! Not really. A venomous poison whispers, "How could God love me? Let's face it, I'm a failure at most things."

For more than ten years after I gave my heart to Christ in that little Pentecostal church, I didn't really believe God loved me. I didn't walk around acknowledging it; that would have been similar to spitting on the crucifix. But in my heart I believed God loved me because it's his job description. He saved my soul because that's what God does for a living. But did he like me? No way. Why would he? What is there to like?

This left me in a continuous state of attempting to perform for God by taking three steps forward and two back. I followed the lead of other Christians and jumped on the exhausting merry-go-round of serving on church committees, attending board meetings, and singing on the worship team in an endeavor to please God. I traded the world's treadmill for the church's treadmill. The only difference was the assurance of eternity in heaven.

Fortunately, God loves me too much to leave me wallowing in lies. Through a long, painful process God revealed that he loves me because he created me. Period. I can't make him love me more, or less. He passionately wants me to fully comprehend that I am deeply, zealously, enthusiastically, and unconditionally loved by the Creator of the universe.

He exposed the villain who stood between us—fear. Fear of trusting, fear of abandonment, fear of rejection were the gatekeepers keeping me from his extravagant love. The decision was up to me. Would I abandon the familiar lies and leap into his embrace? Or would I settle for the frigid slap that performance offered? It all boiled down to trust. My soul knew this was the turning point in my voyage with God.

My whole life changed when I took that jump and let God lavish me with love. With trepidation I allowed him to gently remove the wall of fear that coated my battered heart. That's when I fully understood how my distorted view of God had affected every area of my life.

Please note: If during childhood you had a parent or a circumstance that was abusive, controlling, negligent, absent, or critical, it will have a profound effect on your ability to see God as a loving daddy. But don't be dismayed. Early in life I experienced deep wounds to my soul. My afflictions led me into numerous poor choices (sin or disobedience to God) and destructive decisions. In other words, the sin done to me became the sin done by me. God is willing to heal us emotionally because he longs for the vicious, devastating cycle of depravity to end. If God is able to heal me, he is willing to do the same for you. Isn't it time to seek healing in your own life?

Do you have a distorted view of God? Here are questions that can help:

Do I Believe I Am Loved by God?

Do you know that you make God smile and sing? In the Bible, Zephaniah 3:17[2] says, "He will take great delight in you, he will quiet you with his love, he will rejoice over you with singing." Imagine a toddler charging into the room beaming with excitement and laughter as he rushes into your arms. That's the way God feels. He wants to pick you up with a warm embrace.

Even if I don't feel loved, the truth is I am loved. God taught me this in a very tangible way. When my niece Melissa was born I visited her in the hospital. However, I was not prepared for what happened that day. I wasn't aware that you could fall in love in 2.5 seconds. With one glance it happened—I was smitten. Melissa didn't do anything to earn my adoration. She was wrapped so tightly her little face was the only thing visible. She merely slept and existed. And in an instant I was in love. Dumbfounded, I remember thinking, "This child could murder someone and I would still love her."

When Melissa was nearing her eleventh birthday I reminisced about that first glance. God used that experience to press closely on my heart. It wasn't an audible voice but rather a clear knowing in my soul. He whispered, "Remember how you felt during that first glimpse at Melissa? That's how I feel every time I look at you, Laura."

I gasped—out loud. "What? Seriously? You do?"

By now I assume some readers are thinking, "How do you know that was God?" I understand. The reason I am certain it was God is because my natural tendency is to think otherwise. My natural inclination is to believe his words to me would be, "Listen up; you aren't reading your Bible enough, your prayer life is pathetic, and the other day you treated that waitress like dirt—you'd better start working harder." Not in my wildest thoughts would I imagine him saying, "I'm crazy about you."

And that's why deep in my soul I know that I know that I know it was God's voice. His love pursued me like a starving lion after its prey. Relentless. Fervent. Undeniable. Passionate. Hear God's own words to you: "Because I am God, your personal God, the Holy of Israel, your Savior. I paid a huge price for you. . . . *That's* how much you mean to me! *That's* how much I love you! I'd sell off the whole world to get you back, trade the creation just for you."[3]

Do I Believe God Will Ever Stop Loving Me?

Nothing you have done can cause God to stop loving you. Your response may be, "You don't know the evil I've done." And you are right, I don't. But God does. He may not be pleased with your selfish choices, because he knows they will ultimately bring pain into your life, but that doesn't stop him from loving *you*.

You cannot out-sin his love, but that doesn't mean he winks at sin or ignores disobedient choices. He deeply grieves when we choose our own way over his because it creates a distance between the Creator and his creation. Because his love is perfect, God cannot and will not tolerate disobedience without a consequence. As a truly loving parent he allows an outcome when we disobey. He knows the motivation necessary to stop the destruction and turn us around to do what is wise. His afflictions are never done in malice, cruelty, or impatience but rather in perfect, virtuous love.

Because his unflawed, seamless love is steadfast, it never changes no matter the offense. He always stands willing to forgive. Our job is to humble ourselves, admit the wrong done, apologize to him (and possibly others), ask for forgiveness, and walk toward changing the behavior.

"I've never quit loving you and never will. Expect love, love, and more love!"[4]

Do I Believe God Is Faithful and Will Not Abandon Me?

God is radically different than people. Learning and believing this truth was a huge leap in my spiritual journey. I thought when the going got tough or I did something wrong, God would leave me. That's a lie. He never runs. He is forever faithful. If you have coped with rejection or abandonment this may be a difficult idea to grasp.

My parents' divorce was a traumatic childhood experience that carried into adulthood. The huge fear of the bottom dropping out at any time caused anxiety and a need to control everything. Then in my late twenties the unthinkable happened—my own divorce! My ultimate and most dreaded rejection happened. Even though I knew the Bible said differently, I surmised, "If people reject me, God will too."

During my divorce the tears flowed every day for many months. I thought they were hidden, but I discovered that God saw each one and he collected each precious drop. Psalm 56:8 states, "You have stored my tears in your bottle and counted each of them."[5]

I discovered that his faithfulness is permanent. It is an anchor that never shifts, disappears, or abandons even when the waves threaten to overtake me.

Do I Believe My Value Is Determined by the Price God Paid for Me?

How much are you worth? If you were kidnapped what ransom would you bring? "Not very much," is a typical response. Too often we see our value through the eyes of a parent, spouse, sibling, friend, co-worker, boss, neighbor, or even the dog. It's time to stop the madness and recognize that we are looking in the wrong place for an appraisal. Your price tag has already been stamped by higher standards.

Jesus Christ decided that your value is so significant that he laid down his life to purchase your soul—to ransom you. He decided that you were worth saving. He loves you so much that he wants to spend eternity with you in heaven. This, my friend, is very good news.

Therefore, why do we continue to allow one person's negative opinion determine our worth? Who does God say I am? He says I am a priceless masterpiece (Ephesians 2:10 NLT). He says I am a royal priest (1 Peter 2:9). He says I am the one he loves (Deuteronomy 33:12). He says I am his friend (2 Chronicles 20:7). He says I am beautiful (Isaiah 60:15 NLT).

Why do I believe a person rather than God?

Who Is Your Daddy?

If these questions have been hard for you to answer, do not be discouraged. God wants you to know his complete love even more than you do.

This may be the first time you have ever heard about God's unconditional love and the sacrifice his Son Jesus Christ made to purchase you. If you would like to accept this truth as your own, I suggest beginning with this prayer:

> *Dear God, I'm scared. I think I want to know you but I'm intimidated to take the first step. If the words in this chapter are true I want to know it. It seems too good to be true that I don't have to perform for you to love me. However, I'm learning that even the ability to have faith in you comes from you. So now I open my heart, my mind, and my life to your never-ending love.*
>
> *Thank you for sending your Son Jesus Christ to die on the cross for me. Please forgive me of my sins and help me to walk in newness with you. I desire to know your truth. Thank you for loving me and for teaching me how to have a deeper relationship with you.*
>
> *On my own I am struggling. I need you. Thank you for revealing your love for me. Amen.*

My next suggestion is to begin seeking a community with other people who enjoy the fellowship of God. We were never created to do life alone. This is where finding a stepmom support group in a church can benefit in multiple ways. Or contact www.SisterhoodofStepmoms.com. You can find help and hope.

For the person who has already accepted Jesus, perhaps this chapter has revealed unmistakable hidden lies and profound truths. Here is a prayer for healing.

ಬಾಂ

Holy Papa, there is a part of me that still believes I must perform for you to love me. Help me to let go of the lie. I desire to know your complete, clean, unconditional love in a whole new way.

I'm tired of carrying the load of life's burdens, disappointments, and failures on my own. Teach me how to trust you. Show me how to let go of the pain of my life into your loving arms. I need rest. I need you, Lord—only you. Thank you for loving me. Forgive me for not realizing just how much. Amen.

For God loved the world so much that he gave his one and only Son, so that everyone who believes in him will not perish but have eternal life.

—John 3:16 NLT

It Is Well With My Soul

When peace, like a river, attendeth my way,
When sorrows like sea billows roll;
Whatever my lot, Thou has taught me to say,
It is well, it is well, with my soul.

Refrain:
It is well, with my soul,
It is well, it is well, with my soul.

Though Satan should buffet, though trials should come,
Let this blest assurance control,
That Christ has regarded my helpless estate,
And hath shed His own blood for my soul.

My sin, oh, the bliss of this glorious thought!
My sin, not in part but the whole,
Is nailed to the cross, and I bear it no more,
Praise the Lord, praise the Lord, O my soul!

But, Lord, 'tis for Thee, for Thy coming we wait,
The sky, not the grave, is our goal;
Oh, trump of the angel! Oh, voice of the Lord!
Blessed hope, blessed rest of my soul!

And Lord, haste the day when my faith shall be sight,
The clouds be rolled back as a scroll;
The trump shall resound, and the Lord shall descend,
Even so, it is well with my soul.

Horatio G. Spafford (1873)[6]

Pre-Marriage
Stepfamily Quiz

T his quiz is worded for the potential stepmom. However, those who have already formed a stepfamily will likely discover beneficial insights.

1. How often are you concerned that you and your fiancé have differing core values, priorities, or character traits?

   ☐ Never   ☐ Occasionally   ☐ Frequently   ☐ Always

2. How often does your fiancé have difficulty setting boundaries or allowing consequences for bad behavior with his kids?

   ☐ Never   ☐ Occasionally   ☐ Frequently   ☐ Always

3. How often does your fiancé make decisions regarding his kids out of guilt, fear, anger, or shame?

   ☐ Never   ☐ Occasionally   ☐ Frequently   ☐ Always

4. How often does your fiancé's former spouse have a strong influence over his life, decisions, time, and availability?

   ☐ Never   ☐ Occasionally   ☐ Frequently   ☐ Always

5. How often does your fiancé ignore or make excuses for his children's rudeness or disrespectful attitude?

   ☐ Never   ☐ Occasionally   ☐ Frequently   ☐ Always

6. How often do you find yourself apprehensive, isolated, or retreating when your fiancé's children are around?

☐ Never ☐ Occasionally ☐ Frequently ☐ Always

7. How often do his kids imply that they wish their dad would not remarry?

☐ Never ☐ Occasionally ☐ Frequently ☐ Always

8. How often do you or your fiancé have a negative encounter with the former spouse?

☐ Never ☐ Occasionally ☐ Frequently ☐ Always

9. When you express stepfamily concerns with your fiancé, how often does he dismiss or minimize your feelings or comments?

☐ Never ☐ Occasionally ☐ Frequently ☐ Always

10. How often do you feel angry or frustrated about your fiancé's financial obligations to his children and former spouse?

☐ Never ☐ Occasionally ☐ Frequently ☐ Always

11. How often do you ignore potential problems, or keep issues to yourself, in an effort to keep the peace?

☐ Never ☐ Occasionally ☐ Frequently ☐ Always

12. How often does your fiancé refuse to address the issues that you know are a problem in your forming a stepfamily?

☐ Never ☐ Occasionally ☐ Frequently ☐ Always

13. How often are you concerned that this marriage will negatively affect your own biological children?

☐ Never ☐ Occasionally ☐ Frequently ☐ Always

14. How often does your fiancé blame his former wife for his divorce?

☐ Never ☐ Occasionally ☐ Frequently ☐ Always

15. How often does your fiancé blame you or others rather than take personal responsibility for his poor choices?

☐ Never   ☐ Occasionally   ☐ Frequently   ☐ Always

16. How often do you discover your fiancé has been disloyal or dishonest?

☐ Never   ☐ Occasionally   ☐ Frequently   ☐ Always

17. How often does your fiancé hide or minimize his financial details from you?

☐ Never   ☐ Occasionally   ☐ Frequently   ☐ Always

18. How often do your future in-laws portray or imply that they wish their son would not remarry?

☐ Never   ☐ Occasionally   ☐ Frequently   ☐ Always

If you haven't married yet and you answered "Always" to five or more questions, my suggestion is to take a *big* step backward and evaluate this relationship. Attend a stepfamily workshop, obtain life coaching (both of these can be found on my website, www.TheSmartStepmom.com), or see a therapist who specializes in stepfamilies.

These red flags should not be ignored. Unfortunately, during the dating process most couples convince themselves, "That doesn't really apply to me; our situation will be different."

If you want this marriage to succeed, I suggest taking the steps I mentioned *before* you get married. In the meantime, ask yourself:

- "Am I moving forward because I'm afraid to be alone?"
- "Do I dislike the single life so much that I'm minimizing serious issues?"
- "Why am I ignoring red flags?"
- "Have I truly considered how this marriage will affect my kids, his kids, and our future?"
- "Why am I afraid to put this marriage on hold?"

If you are already a stepmom and this quiz stirred some anguish, you may be muttering, "Okay, I ignored the warning signs and my home is in chaos, now what do I do?"

First, don't lose heart. I was one of those stepmoms too. There is help and hope. The important thing is to resist the urge to deny the seriousness of your issues. Here are a few steps to take:

- Get counseling from someone who understands stepfamilies, even if it's a financial challenge. The average uncontested divorce starts at $10,000. Take my word for it; the investment in counseling is worth it!

- Attend a workshop or event for stepmoms and/or stepfamilies, even if your spouse won't attend—you go. Visit www.SisterhoodofStepmoms.com for more information.

- Read resources on children of divorce or adult children of divorce.

- Life coaching is sometimes a great option. Many of my life coaching clients tell me it did more for them than counseling because I ask questions that dive into the root causes of the problem. Plus I grew up in a stepfamily, and I've been a stepmom for twenty-eight years. Contact me at laura@laurapetherbridge.com.

- Read the two chapters in *The Smart Stepmom* written for the dad with your spouse. These chapters were specifically designed to open the doors of communication on fragile and tender topics.

Stepmom, don't be discouraged, depressed, or disheartened. You can do it. I know you can!

Notes

Chapter 1: Why Is It So Complicated?

1. Phillip C. McGraw, PhD, *Life Strategies* (New York: Hyperion, 1999), 109.
2. Jen Abbas, *Generation Ex: Adult Children of Divorce and the Healing of Our Pain* (Colorado Springs: Waterbrook, 2004), 86.
3. www.DivorceCare.org, www.GriefShare.org, www.CelebrateRecovery.org
4. From a personal conversation with Heather Hetchler, founder, www.Cafe Smom.com. Used with permission.

Chapter 2: When Your Hubby Is Stuck: Stepmom Frustration

1. Judith S. Wallerstein, Julia M. Lewis, and Sandra Blakeslee, *The Unexpected Legacy of Divorce* (New York: Hyperion, 2000), xxxiii.

Chapter 3: Will We Ever Get Along?—The Ex-Wife-in-Law

1. "The Second Wife: Baptized by Barf," *Stepmom Magazine,* May 2013, www. stepmommagazine.com.
2. Reinhold Niebuhr, *The Essential Reinhold Niebuhr,* ed. Robert McAfee Brown (New Haven, CT: Yale University Press, 1986), 251.
3. Lara R. Badain, Esq., "How to Avoid Unnecessary Legal Headaches With Your Ex-Wife," *Stepmom Magazine,* June 2013, 9, www.stepmommagazine.com.

Chapter 4: The Full-Time Stepmom—When Mom Is Missing

1. Dr. Archibald Hart, *Helping Children Survive Divorce* (Dallas: Word Publishing, 1996), 20.
2. Ibid., 92.
3. www.goodreads.com/author/quotes/1148687.Samuel_Chadwick

Chapter 7: "What Did You Say?" Educating Family and Friends

1. Paul Coughlin and Jennifer D. Degler, PhD, *No More Christian Nice Girl* (Bloomington, MN: Bethany House, 2010), 52.

2. Proverbs 27:17

Chapter 8: Holidays, Weddings, Mother's Day—Oh My!

1. Ron Deal and Laura Petherbridge, *The Smart Stepmom* (Bloomington, MN: Bethany House, 2009), 206.

Chapter 9: Let's Hear It From the Men—Hubby's Perspective

1. Ron Deal and Laura Petherbridge, *The Smart Stepmom* (Bloomington, MN: Bethany House, 2009), 132.

2. Ibid., 106.

3. Heather Hetchler with Andy Hetchler, "Hard Times Loop: One Man's Perspective on Stepfamily Life," *StepMom Magazine,* June 2013, 17, www.step mommagazine.com.

Chapter 10: Mirror, Mirror on the Wall—A Peek Inside

1. Henry Cloud and John Townsend, *Boundaries in Marriage* (Grand Rapids, MI: Zondervan, 1999), 32.

2. Pat Springle, *Rapha's Twelve-Step Program for Overcoming Codependency* (Houston and Dallas: Rapha, 1990), 13. Quoted in Laura Petherbridge, *When "I Do" Becomes "I Don't"* (Colorado Springs, CO: David C. Cook, 2008), 116.

3. Rick Warren, *The Purpose-Driven Life* (Grand Rapids, MI: Zondervan, 2002), 153.

4. Phillip C. McGraw, PhD, *Life Strategies* (New York: Hyperion, 1999), 109.

5. Warren, *The Purpose-Driven Life*, 153.

6. List adapted from Laura Petherbridge, *When "I Do" Becomes "I Don't"* (Colorado Springs, CO: David C. Cook, 2008), 117.

7. John P. Splinter, *The Complete Divorce Recovery Handbook* (Grand Rapids, MI: Zondervan, 1992), 83.

Chapter 11: Who's Your Daddy? Satisfying Our Deepest Longing

1. John 14:6
2. NIV 1984
3. Isaiah 43:3–4 THE MESSAGE
4. Jeremiah 31:3 THE MESSAGE
5. CEV
6. Public domain, fourth stanza removed.

Laura Petherbridge is an international speaker, author of *When "I Do" Becomes "I Don't": Practical Steps for Healing During Separation and Divorce*, and coauthor of *The Smart Stepmom*. She has been featured on *Focus on the Family, FamilyTalk with Dr. James Dobson*, Moody Broadcasting, and *FamilyLife Today*. Laura has spoken at the Billy Graham Training Center and is a featured expert on the DivorceCare DVD series used by more than 12,000 churches worldwide. Laura is a regular contributor to *Stepmom Magazine* (a non-faith-based publication), *MomLife Today*, and *Family Matters Magazine*. Her written work has also appeared in Christianity Today's *Marriage Partnership, Lifeway Magazine, Today's Christian Woman,* and on Crosswalk.com.

Laura and her husband, Steve, reside in Summerfield, Florida. Visit her at www.TheSmartStepmom.com or www.Sisterhood ofStepmoms.com.

More Tips for the Smart Stepfamily

More stepmom help from Laura Petherbridge!
Because the role of stepmom can be confusing and lonely, Laura Petherbridge teamed up with leading blended family expert Ron Deal to offer the hope, encouragement, and practical advice women need to survive *and thrive* as a stepmom.

The Smart Stepmom by Ron L. Deal and Laura Petherbridge
thesmartstepmom.com

The top guide to building a smart stepfamily—now revised and expanded!
Providing practical, realistic solutions to the unique issues that stepfamilies face, Ron Deal helps remarried couples solve the everyday challenges of stepparenting and shares seven steps to raising a healthy family.

The Smart Stepfamily by Ron L. Deal
smartstepfamilies.com